Where were you when President Kennedy was shot?

Memories and Tributes
to a Slain President
as Told to

DEAR ABBY

Foreword by Pierre Salinger

Andrews and McMeel
A Universal Press Syndicate Company
Kansas City

Design by Barrie Maguire

Library of Congress Cataloging-in-Publication Data

Where were you when President Kennedy was shot? :
    memories and tributes to a slain president, as told
    to Dear Abby / foreword by Pierre Salinger.
        p.   cm.
    ISBN 0-8362-6246-8 : $6.95
    1. Kennedy, John F. (John Fitzgerald), 1917-1963—
Assassination. 2. American letters.   I. Van Buren,
Abigail.
E842.9.W45   1993
973.922—dc20   93-27360
                                                          CIP

FOR THE
KENNEDY FAMILY

Contents

Foreword

It is fascinating that almost thirty years after John F. Kennedy was assassinated, so many people around the world remember exactly where they were and how they reacted to his death. I found it extraordinary that three hundred thousand persons had responded to Abigail Van Buren's column asking for her readers' recollections.

For me, it was a dramatic day. I had left the White House on November 19 to accompany six members of JFK's cabinet to an economic conference in Tokyo. President Kennedy had asked me to join the trip to organize his visit to Tokyo, planned for February 1964. This would have been the first visit by an American president to Japan since the end of World War II.

We stopped in Honolulu for three days for an important meeting on the Vietnam crisis. Early in the morning of November 22, the White House plane headed for Tokyo. I was in the back of the plane reading the economic papers when suddenly somebody came and told me the six cabinet secretaries had to see me. They were in the office in the front of the plane. When I walked in it was grim. They handed me a wire bulletin saying Kennedy had been shot.

The plane turned around and headed back to Honolulu, and I was instructed to take over the communications system to the White House and find out what had happened. When I connected with the White House, there was total confusion. For many minutes nothing was coming through clearly. About a half hour after the plane had turned around, I heard in my ear: "Wayside. Standby."

Wayside was my code name. About every thirty seconds for the next five minutes, I heard the same thing. Then suddenly came a new message. "Wayside. Lancer is dead." Lancer was the code name for President Kennedy.

I was destroyed. I so admired and liked JFK. I had a feeling that not only was he lost, but that my life was lost.

When we reached Washington, a car took me to the White House. JFK's body had just arrived in the East Room and there was a short prayer service. Jackie Kennedy came up to me after the prayer and said I had had a terrible day and should sleep in the White House.

I went upstairs where I talked with colleagues like Ken O'Donnell and Larry O'Brien until five in the morning. Finally, I went to sleep.

At 7 A.M. the phone rang. I heard the operator say: "Mr. Salinger, the president wants to talk to you." For an instant, I thought I'd had a nightmare. Then, on the phone I heard: "Pierre, this is Lyndon." It was over. It was now clear to me that Kennedy was dead.

I hope many people will read this book and understand what a world-wide influence John Kennedy had at the time of his assassination. Nearly thirty years after his death, people have not forgotten him or his contribution to our country and the world.

I salute Abigail Van Buren for this memorable project.

—PIERRE SALINGER

Preface

We all have experienced at least one moment in our lives that is literally unforgettable. If you were at least four years old in November of 1963, you will never forget where you were when you heard the news that President Kennedy had been shot.

I remember that day as though it were yesterday: My husband and I were vacationing in Japan with our good friends Stanley Mosk and his wife, Edna (now deceased). Mosk was California's attorney general at the time.

We were at the Okura Hotel in Tokyo. At four A.M., Mosk received a telephone call from his office in the States—delivering the terrible news that President Kennedy had been assassinated in Dallas! We turned on our television sets and saw the same newscasts that were being beamed all over the world. We were numb and heartsick.

Every Japanese person we encountered in the corridors, the elevator, and the lobby of our hotel bowed his head respectfully and said softly with genuine remorse, "So sorry about your president. . . ."

For all intents and purposes, our vacation had ended; we were no longer in the mood to sightsee and have a good time. Other American tourists in Tokyo felt as we did . . . we just wanted to go "home" and be with our people. And so we did.

Exactly thirty years later, I ran the following note in my column: "Where were you when you heard that President Kennedy had been shot? Please respond briefly; postcards preferred." I wisely rented a post office box so these postcards would be separate from the routine "Dear Abby" mail, but I was not prepared for the deluge that was to come!

I received over 300,000 responses and devoted several columns sharing those responses with my readers, but as the recollections continued to come in, it became obvious that a column or two could not do justice to that historic remembrance.

Mail came from small towns and major cities—from Alaska to the Philippines, from Berlin to Africa. Your recollections were fascinating, humorous, and heartwarming.

There were the inevitable theories of why and how, a spattering of negative anecdotes, tales of ESP and premonitions, but the majority of responses were moving tributes to our slain president.

Although this was the beginning of a violent chapter in American history, your responses reflect a simpler time— a time when children came home from school for lunch; women ironed a lot; male and female college students lived in separate dormitories; and families watched black and white TVs.

Many of you said that you looked forward to reading what others were doing on that fateful day. Several of you expressed the hope that your old classmate, the teacher you admired, the neighbor who brought you the news, or the stranger you wept with would read and remember, too. It soon became clear that I had to share those recollections with you.

The following chapters represent some of the more unusual and touching stories. Many are strikingly similar, only mailed from a different town or another country. Some reflect the routine of everyday life, others tell of a unique or special event.

You will read stories graphically related by people who are now in their eighties and nineties, also recollections labeled "my first childhood memory" by those presumed to have been too young to remember. From their descriptions, you can almost see the moss green ribbon being wrapped around a Christmas ornament; the cozy window seat; the child sitting in the third row from the front in a junior high school classroom; the "Happy Birthday" sign tearfully being taken down; and the flag being lowered to half-mast over the Capitol Building.

We all have experienced moments in our lives that are literally unforgettable, but rarely are they shared by others outside of our families or circle of close friends.

The recollections in this book reflect on a moment shared by millions of people who will never forget where they were on November 22, 1963, when they heard the news that President Kennedy had been shot.

—ABIGAIL VAN BUREN

1.

I'll Never Forget

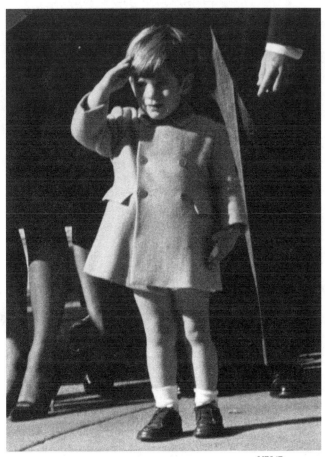

DEAR ABBY: *Amazingly we share the same memory of President Kennedy's assassination! Did we by any chance share the same hotel? I was staying at the Okura Hotel in Tokyo. I still have the* Stars and Stripes *issued that day in Japan detailing the tragedy. I wonder if you were one of the Americans we met that day as we all sought to share our shock and grief?*

R.B.J., SEATTLE, WA

November 22, 1963, is the date I was conceived. Apparently my parents sought comfort in each other after hearing the news. I was born August 29, 1964. My mom confessed this to me only last year!

C., SPRINGFIELD, MA

My family was still in my hometown, Sighet, North Romania, divided from the Soviet Union only by a short wooden bridge. We were desperately awaiting our passports to be able to leave the Communist "Eden."

About the assassination of President John F. Kennedy, we learned only the next night from the emissions of Free Europe radio station—at that time a very dangerous risk! Our anguish of ever being able to reach the shores of America became even worse.

Our nice dreams materialized three years later when we did reach the shores of the New World, but this could be described only in a separate story.

C.K., SEMINOLE, FL

I could *see* the bad news travel up and down the aisles of the supermarket—it was uncanny. The scene remains as vivid in memory as the day it happened. J.A.W., SEATTLE, WA

I was just six years old in afternoon kindergarten. Our principal's voice came over the loudspeaker, announcing that the president had been shot. Our teacher was crying and the principal's voice was heavy with sadness. I walked home to find my mother watching television. I think everyone in my hometown of Wapakoneta, Ohio, was watching Walter Cronkite on their black and white TVs. I remembered thinking that Walter Cronkite sounded sad and near tears, just like the principal. I looked at little Caroline, and wondered what it would be like to lose your daddy at our age. E.S., COLUMBUS, OH

I was being stopped for speeding. When the police- man arrived at my window, I told him the president had been shot, to get in and listen to the radio. He did so and in a few minutes departed; issuance of a ticket was not mentioned. A.L., ROGERSVILLE, TN

I was military attache in the American Embassy in Mogadishu, Somalia. When I arrived home I found anxious friends, Somalis, members of the international community, and people from international agencies waiting for information, sharing the grief, and providing mutual support. The next day, a memorial book was placed in the embassy lobby. Through the "bush telegraph" Somali tribesman out in the bush heard of the tragedy and many walked miles in the heat across the desert to make their mark or sign their name in the book. There was also a requiem mass. The church and courtyard were packed with members of the various embassy staffs, the international community, and Muslim Somalis, all paying their last respects. M.L.C., ANACORTES, WA

I was three weeks overdue during my last pregnancy when I heard the president had been shot. A few hours later I was on my way to the hospital where I delivered twins!

I spent all that night on an emotional roller coaster; plunging to the depths of sorrow, weeping over the death of my president, then soaring to the heights of elated joy, laughing over the births of my beautiful daughters.

During my stay at the hospital, there was not the noisy "hustle and bustle" usually heard in the corridors. Patients kept to their rooms and the nurses and staff slowly and quietly went about their duties; everybody keeping an ear close to a radio or TV, trying to comprehend the awful truth.

I will always remember the turmoil I felt then; the horrible shock at John Kennedy's senseless death, and the wondrous joy at Judy's and Jenny's unexpected twin births.

On that memorable day, God took away someone important in my life. Then he blessed me twice.

C.J., BLUE SPRINGS, MO

Prologue: *In 1945 when Roosevelt died, I was at our Signal Company in Foggia, Italy. I decided to wake my sergeant to listen to the radio and help circulate the news.*

On November 22, 1963, I was attending a seminar in Chicago. The same sergeant was sitting next to me when the news from Dallas unfolded. He turned to me and said, "We have to stop meeting like this."

B.C., PARK RIDGE, IL

I had just purchased two power tools for my husband's Christmas present. He uses the tools to this day, and every time I hear them it brings back a feeling of hurt, despair, and of the great loss to our country. C.M., INDIANAPOLIS, IN

My husband was stationed at Fort Campbell, Kentucky. On that unforgettable day, he was away on maneuvers and would be gone several days. I was five months pregnant with my first child, and alone in a strange city. Watching TV, I heard the announcement, "President Kennedy has been shot."

I continued to listen, and became more and more afraid. I dropped my dinner plate and walked five miles to the only person I knew in Tennessee. We sat and cried for hours. We didn't know what else to do. I don't think I've ever been more scared and devastated in my life. Since then I've lost a husband (age thirty-two) and a son (age eighteen).

Even as I write this, I am crying; it's as though it happened yesterday. I've never seen our nation rally together as it did on that day. It was a time I'll never forget. C.D., PORTLAND, OR

I was in the Peace Corps and had been teaching English in a small town in Thailand for just two months. The shy young Thai student who lived with me came and told me in Thai that President Kennedy had died. I couldn't imagine why he would die suddenly, and said, "Oh, you must mean that his father has died." No, no, she said, and kept explaining in Thai what had happened. I didn't know the Thai word for "assassinate," so I couldn't understand her. Finally, she got her English lesson book and pointed to a drawing of a fellow shooting a gun, next to the sentence, "He fired a shot." Then I knew. M.J.B., VAN NUYS, CA

Heading home from downtown Oakland, California, the bus passed the Oakland Tribune Building and a newsboy was shouting, "President Assassinated." Sitting across from me was a very large black lady with a heart even larger as she cried, "Dear Lord. Mercy, no Lord. I loved that man so much!" Such a genuine expression of love and despair, one can't easily forget, and as she wept, we all were crying.

B.V., FOLSOM, CA

My most aching memory is the sight of Caroline fumbling under the flag to touch the coffin while she prayed. K.A., LAKEWOOD, CO

How could I forget? I had gone to the grocery store, where I heard the shocking news. I rushed home immediately to find my dear husband slumped in his chair—dead of a massive heart attack! The radio beside him was still blasting. L.M., PHOENIX, AZ

I was in Times Square in New York City. All the lights on the "Great White Way" were darkened. The only lights were around the old Times Building on the running headlines that the president had been shot. People were hugging and crying. Times Square was a lot different in those days and definitely different that day. G.M., ASTORIA, NY

> **I** *was in the midst of an IRS audit when the news came. They said, "Forget it. Case dismissed!" The combination of elation and sadness has never left me.*
>
> ALTOONA, PA

I was studying in the law library in the U.S. Senate when I heard that President Kennedy had been shot. I rushed across the hall and into the Senate gallery, just in time to see Senator Ted Kennedy, then a freshman senator, hurriedly leave the presiding

8

officer's chair on the Senate floor. He had an unforgettable, ashen look of horror on his face.

I then reported for roll call at the U.S. Capitol Police Force where I was a "rookie." I, along with another young fellow Montanan, were instructed to lower the United States flag to half-mast. As we were on the roof, tears were streaming from our eyes. We looked down and saw hundreds of cars parked on various streets leading to the Capitol, with the occupants standing beside them, looking up at us and weeping. D.C.R., BUTTE, MT

O ur eight-year-old daughter came home from school and asked what was going on. When told the president was shot in Texas she said with wide eyes, "Was it *cowboys*?" J., BETHLEHEM, PA

O n November 22, I was a comatose patient at L&M Hospital in New London, Connecticut. I was not aware of the assassination until a few weeks later when I began to recover. I missed the single most publicized event of my lifetime. How many others can say that! M.J.C., WATERFORD, CT

I had an unusual experience. When I heard the news about President Kennedy and also his brother Robert Kennedy, I happened to be in the same place—

a beauty shop in Netcong, New Jersey, sitting under a hair dryer. F.W., WILDWOOD, FL

I was standing in the County Courthouse in Redwood City, California, waiting to be sworn in as a citizen of the U.S.A. The judge announced that due to the tragic events of the day, he was dispensing with all ceremonies, so "Please raise your right hand. Welcome to the United States." B.O., PARADISE, CA

There was never a more dismal scene than on the streets of Washington that day and in particular around the White House and Capitol Building. People crying, a gloom hung in the air. I went to the funeral procession and the sound of hearing those drums and the horses' hoofs AND NO OTHER SOUND—TOTAL QUIET—is still in my mind.

P.K.Y., DUNMORE, PA

It was my twelfth birthday. My father was weeping in his room. My mother tried valiantly to give a birthday party for seven bewildered twelve-year-old girls. I spent that Thanksgiving weekend sadly watching the funeral on TV. I sobbed when John John saluted. Our grief was overwhelming. It was the end of an age of innocence. That gut-wrenching experience was brought back to me four years ago when I buried my father at Arlington Cemetery. A retired colonel, he was buried with the same horse-drawn caisson, marching band, gun salute, and taps. For many years, when asked my birthday people would remark, "That's the day Kennedy was shot!" I am forty-one now. Few, if any remark on the date, but I will never forget. K.A., SEBASTOPOL, CA

Instead of dwelling on that heartbreaking day in Dallas, I wish Americans would remember the intelligence, the warmth, courage, and humor John Kennedy gave us for a thousand shining days.
M.B., SEATTLE, WA

When I first heard that President Kennedy was shot, I was a fifth grade student. The custodian came into our room and announced that the president and governor of Texas had been shot! My reaction: "I didn't know Texas had a president! Why doesn't Ohio have one too?"

We were dismissed from school and the local Christmas Parade was canceled. I was thrilled since the fifth grade band had to march.

My friend came over to my house after school and

11

we watched a news reporter talk about the assassination. After a few minutes, we went outside to watch our new neighbors move in, and wondered as a plane flew over, if it carried the President and Mrs. Kennedy back to Washington. S.Z., ST. CLAIRSVILLE, OH

One of my very first memories is the day JFK was shot. I was three years, ten months old. My mother took me to Sears "uptown" in Youngstown, Ohio. We were in the appliance department, and I saw all these rows of TV sets all turned on. Suddenly the same thing came on all the sets. "President Kennedy shot in Dallas." A large crowd gathered. People wept. We watched it all on TV for a week. I think my mom cried every day. C.H.B., LISBON, OH

I was appearing in court in Whittier, California, on a traffic ticket. The judge fined me fifty dollars, and as I stood in line to pay, an aide came to the bench and notified her of the events of the day. She dismissed all the remaining cases. I was the last to pay a fine that day. E.W., THOUSAND PALMS, CA

I was in an autograph dealer's apartment in Brooklyn. After we heard that President Kennedy had been shot, he

*went to his files and pulled out all his
L.B.J. signatures which had automati-
cally increased in value.*

G.H.W., FAIR LAWN, NJ

I stood on a corner watching the parade. President
Kennedy and Mrs. Kennedy were given a tremen-
dous welcome in Dallas. I was about twenty feet
from their Lincoln Continental. I was overjoyed and
cheered them along.

I went back to the office after the cars passed.
When I got up there we started hearing sirens everywhere, from every direction. One of the guys had a
radio and said that President Kennedy had been shot
and was taken to Parkland Hospital. Everyone felt so
sad, and especially that it happened in Dallas.

By the way, the next day the entire knoll was
covered with flowers and words of bereavement.
L.E.M., HURST, TX

I t was my daughter's wedding day. The wedding
had been postponed for two weeks due to a death
in the family. The groom-to-be said, "We're getting
married tomorrow come hell or high water."

The next day after we heard the news, *the rains
came.* So you see, his words came true. They got
married *despite* hell *and* high water. E.M.D., BRAZORIA, TX

13

On November 22, 1963, my Argentine husband was listening to the news with colleagues in his office in Buenos Aires. The announcement of President Kennedy's death struck them speechless. Political assassination in the United States! Of a president they liked and admired. They stared at each other without finding words. B.S.M., AUSTIN, TX

I am a native Washingtonian and rolled my eggs on the White House lawn every Easter Monday, but had never been inside. On November 22, 1963, I was waiting in the tourist line to go in with my two small daughters and mother. Imagine how shocked we were when we heard the news!! I've never been inside and I now live in Virginia. M.M., LURAY, VA

I was on the operating table in the middle of a hemorrhoidectomy when a nurse rushed in and shouted, "Doctor, I just heard that President Kennedy was shot in Dallas!" The doctor dropped the instrument he was holding and gasped, "Oh, my God!" I was left in a jackknife position until he regained his composure, after which he completed the surgery with somewhat unsteady hands. Later, the informer stuck her head in the room and said, "Sorry, Doctor, I guess that news could have waited." To which he replied, "It sure as hell could have!" ATLANTA, GA

. . . I'll Never Forget

I was fifteen years old and a freshman in high school. Students were crying and seemed dazed. We had a quick tearful assembly and were let out early. I remember a feeling of loneliness and emptiness. My mother had died the month before and I still was hurting very badly from that. I remember wondering if they now knew each other. I was afraid of what might happen to our country. S.N., PORTLAND, OR

I was on an American Airlines jet flying from NYC to LA. I was looking out the window at the great sights of Washington, D.C., when the pilot came on the P.A. system and said, "I regret to inform you that President John F. Kennedy is dead." Near Nashville, the pilot pointed out the airplane carrying the president's body back to Washington. E.W., KNOXVILLE, TN

I was in labor and gave birth to our third son "John Fitzgerald" just minutes after they made the announcement. We were all in such a state of shock. The doctor held our baby in his arms and with tears in his eyes called him little John, after the president. J.T., OGDEN, UT

I was walking from the cafeteria to the classroom in a Birmingham, Alabama, junior high school. When it was first announced, I remember some kids laugh-

ing and clapping (remember Kennedy had re-molded southern institutions). Within the hour it was announced that he had died. We were all overwhelmed, and then I remember how hard and uncontrollably I cried. We had a time for silent prayers. Nobody seemed to know what to do next—it was as if time stood still.

B.K., TRUSSVILLE, AL

USC's dental clinic, where twenty-four students were working on patients. Twenty-four dental instruments were held skyward and forty-eight mouths opened simultaneously—forty-nine including my own. E., LONG BEACH, CA

I went to the funeral—ended up on a private porch opposite the church. I remember seeing de Gaulle (so tall), Prince Philip (so handsome), Selassie (so tiny)—but what I remember most is the shocked, hurt expression in the eyes of everyone. The world has never been the same.

G.C., ORMOND BEACH, FL

2.

I Was at Home

DEAR ABBY: *I was down on my knees scrubbing my kitchen floor when I heard the terrible news about our president. It made a good position for prayer.*

S.P., NEW HAVEN, CT

My wife was pregnant with our fourth child and we were building our dream home in the country. On that particular afternoon, I had just finished planting six birch trees on one side of our long driveway when a colleague drove in to tell me the news of the president's assassination. Incidentally, all of the trees died within six months! R.E.E., BONN, GERMANY

On November 22, 1963, I was getting ready for my wedding. We married at 7:30 that night and spent the weekend watching all the events. My birthday is the same as Jackie's and I was in almost the same pink suit and hat. J.R.W., FLATORIA, TX

Dingdong! The Avon lady told me. She had just heard it at a previous call. She stayed, and together we watched TV for details. B., NEWARK, DE

Iwas married in January 1963 and was living in the Chicago suburbs—five hundred miles from my family.

My husband's job involved constant travel, and he was gone the weekend President Kennedy was killed. I was six weeks away from delivering our first child, and felt very isolated and very much alone with my grief. C.S., MINNETONKA, MN

It was with great delight I watched the president and Jackie charm Texas. Around 11:30, I went out to my front porch to look for my children coming home for lunch. My neighbor was screeching, "The president has been shot." It took a few minutes for me to absorb her dreadful news. It took *years* for my tears to dry. C.M., NEWTON, MA

My grandmother always kept two portraits in her home—the Pope and Kennedy.

E.A.F., HUNTSVILLE, AL

That evening, my father, a staunch Republican, put our house flagpole at half-staff and put a light on it so the flag would be seen twenty-four hours a day for the whole week. C.A.A., EMMAUS, PA

I am seventy years young. I will never forget the year 1963. I was standing on a chair in my kitchen washing the walls down when my daughter returned home from school and told me President Kennedy was dead. It was a very terrible and sad moment in my life. A.B., BAYONNE, NJ

I had just gotten home from the hospital after a failed suicide attempt. I was twenty. Like JFK, I'm a Gemini and understand his dark moody side. This seemed so significant that whenever I wanted to give up, I hung in there to defy "destiny." Thirty years later I'm still plugging away. D.T., BISBEE, AZ

On the day our beloved president, John Kennedy, was wastefully assassinated, I was at home with my four young children. I had set up my ironing board in the living room. Believe me, there wasn't any steam needed from my iron, as my tears wet each piece sufficiently. It was truly one of the saddest days in my life. C.L., LINCOLN, NE

On November 22, 1963, my son who was fifteen years old, my two daughters, aged thirteen and five, myself, and family and friends had just returned from my husband's funeral. As we started to eat, I received a phone call telling me the president had been shot. Needless to say we all grieved again as if he were a member of our family. I can never forget that doubly sad day. M.K., BAYONNE, NJ

I was working at a new job in a new city where I knew no one. I went home to an unfamiliar apartment with no one to share my grief. It was the day before my twenty-first birthday—the loneliest weekend of my life.

L., MICHIGAN

The washing machine repairman arrived at our door. His first words were, "Did you hear Kennedy was assassinated?" I gave him a withering look of disgust at his tasteless comment and replied, "Okay, what's the joke?" Like the rest of the nation we were glued to the TV day and night for the next two weeks, but I'll never forget that indelible moment and my glib response. P.G., MANHATTAN BEACH, CA

We began a vigil of endless television coverage on a small black-and-white set. Mother never sat idle so she asked me to teach her how to knit something simple. We decided on a white cotton dish-cloth. We watched the assassination, Oswald's death, Ruby's arrest, the funeral mass, and the burial. Meanwhile, Mom knit a dishrag five feet long. I guess I

21

should have taught her how to bind off. We call it the "Kennedy Rag." L.L., DULUTH, MN

I was scrubbing and waxing my dining room floors in preparation for Thanksgiving and my husband's return from school in Champaign, Illinois. After I heard the news, I hardly had the heart to finish the job. F.R., ST. LOUIS, MO

I was changing my daughter's diaper when I heard President Kennedy had been shot. I instantly thought of Jackie and the fact that she'd lost her baby, which had been due about the same time as my daughter, and now she was losing her husband! J.L., MELBOURNE, FL

On the day President Kennedy was shot, my father and I were planting a Norway Maple seedling in my front yard. As we were pressing the soil in around the tree, my neighbor came out and shouted to us, "The president has been shot." This tree has grown to be a beautiful shade tree and a living memorial to President Kennedy.

E.K., TOWACO, NJ

I was outside on a stepladder, washing my front windows when my sister-in-law called to me, "The president has been shot." I put the ladder away, went into the house, turned on the TV, closed the drapes, and cried for the next four days. N.W., SPARTANBURG, SC

My husband had left me to live with another woman after a secret love affair with her, and an abusive relationship with me. I was packing the rest of his things, when a person came rushing to my door saying excitedly, "Somebody shot him, somebody shot him." After regaining my senses, all I could say was, "Who?" NO NAME

I heard of the assassination of President Kennedy while I was holding on the telephone with J.C. Penney's to check on a bedroom furniture delivery. When the girl came back on the phone, she told me the shocking news. In the middle of the mundane routine of living. . . . H.T., LEVITTOWN, NY

I was standing by the ironing board ironing and memorizing the solo I would be singing at church Sunday, "O Joyous Day." The organist called and said, "Of course you will want to do a different solo won't you? Kennedy has been shot, fatally they think." I was devastated, heartsick, and sad. E.K., KANSAS CITY, MO

Dear Abby . . .

It was near noon and I was cleaning pheasants. I'm sure I washed them in water mingled with tear drops. G.A., DULUTH, MN

I was home packing for a trip to Austin where the president was to appear that night. I still have the tickets for that dinner. His death was somehow more shocking to me because I saw President Kennedy the night before at a dinner in Houston. J.P., HOUSTON, TX

I was in my kitchen in St. Paul, Minnesota, giving my friend Marge a Toni Home Permanent. We were stunned to hear that President Kennedy had been assassinated, and during the final conditioner application, that he had died. H.H., ST. PAUL, MN

On November 22, 1963, I was in my kitchen making cranberry sauce for Thanksgiving from cranberries our family had gathered that October from a small boggy patch among the sand dunes on Cape Cod. My neighbor came running over, tears streaming down her face, sobbing the news. We stood together by the sunny window, hugging each other and crying until my sons came home from school, each wide-eyed and wondering what it meant that the president of our country was killed. It was a sad, sad day for all of us. R.B., MERIDEN, CT

24

. . . I Was at Home

I was a young wife and mother standing in my apartment kitchen grinding up some leftover roast beef to make hash for dinner. My neighbor came over and told me President Kennedy had been shot. Our English neighbors upstairs came down. The wife was crying, saying, "How could this happen in America?" We were all so shocked and sad.

B.R.J., VALENCIA, PA

My sister-in-law and I were on her kitchen floor tacking an old-fashioned quilt, when her neighbor came running in screaming and crying, "The president's just been shot. He's dead!" We stopped working, turned on the radio and listened. Abby, to this day I don't know what happened to that quilt or if we even finished it! L.J., HANANA, AR

Our milkman had just delivered our milk, and told me our president was assassinated. Twenty minutes later, someone told me our milkman's truck had overturned and crushed him! Two tragedies within half hour. H.W., TACOMA, WA

My father came home for lunch. As he got out of the car I approached him begging for any candy or gum from his pockets. He uncharacteristically ignored me, seeming preoccupied. Perplexed by his brush off, I followed him into the house where he announced the dreadful news. Five weeks later I turned eight years old. I vividly recall my birthday wish: "Please God, somehow bring President Kennedy back to life." P.T., BERKELEY, CA

I remember hearing the news while cleaning my kitchen. My husband was out in the garage. It was such sad news we both thought it was like the end of the world. The president was so well liked. When I think of it, I still feel bad. I'm a widow now, and my husband has been gone ten years. Time does heal some. Thank God.

T.D., ST. LOUIS, MO

3.

I Was in the Military

DEAR ABBY: I was a junior naval officer. We had finished our crossing of the Atlantic Ocean, had passed through the Straits of Gibraltar, and were anchored in a protected bay in the Balearic Islands. An announcement came over the ship's loudspeaker system that our president and commander in chief, John F. Kennedy had been shot and killed. It was a devastating moment in my young life as President Kennedy represented youth, vigor, and hope to my generation. The news of his death choked me up. I wanted to cry. Here I was so far from home and family, and I really felt the sadness, grief, and the loneliness.

We held a memorial service. Our whole fleet was present. We watched as a wreath was laid on the sea in honor and memory of our gallant ex-navy president. What a feeling of patriotism I felt then! D.E.G., STEVENSON, AL

My husband, an air force career man, and I were living in England when our dear President John F. Kennedy was killed. It's bad—but in a foreign land it's even worse. The British people were very kind, very sympathetic, but it would have been better to be at home (U.S.A.) at the time. L., PINE BLUFF, AR

I had just awakened to my first day in Vietnam. I was twenty years old. B.S., SAN JOSE, CA

We were stationed in Vicenza, Italy. The outpouring of sympathy from our Italian neighbors was overwhelming. Hundreds of students marched to the Army post carrying huge wreaths of flowers. I have tears in my eyes as I write this. M.M.B., BUFFALO, NY

I was a soldier secretary in West Berlin, Germany. Many soldiers were stunned, some cried, some got mad, some walked around in a daze, some even got into fights. All military installations were immediately closed, all non-Americans were escorted off the post. SPRINGFIELD, MO

My air force husband and I were eating dinner at 6:20 p.m. (Paris time) in our U.S. military housing unit near Evreux AFB in northern France. A neighbor came to our door to tell us the shocking news that was being reported on Armed Forces Radio about President Kennedy's assassination. We turned on our radio (we had no televisions or telephones in our units), and listened in stunned silence. Shortly, neighbors began to gather in our home. Some listened to the continuing radio news reports, some sat silently in the living room nodding to each other, some of the men spoke in hushed tones in the kitchen. We all needed to share our shock, our disbelief, and our total sadness that night so far away from the U.S.A. M.T.C., DALLAS, TX

Midday on November 22, 1963, I was performing a spinal operation on a marine during a tour of duty as a neurosurgeon at the Oakland Naval Hospital in California. A medical corpsman entered the operating room and said, "Sir, the president has just been shot." I could not believe his message—the president seemed so alive and vibrant, at the height of the "Camelot" era—and besides, navy people tended to identify very positively with the former C.O. of PT Boat 109.

Somehow the surgical team finished its work that day, but we were hardly able to comprehend what we had heard. That night navy ships in San Francisco Bay began firing one cannon round every hour in honor of the slain president. This custom, I was told, dated back to the assassination of President Lincoln. It went on, night and day, until Jack Kennedy was buried. Those muffled booms were the saddest sounds I ever heard.

M.W., TACOMA, WA

...I Was in the Military

It's a day I'll never forget! I was in North Kingston, Rhode Island, a military wife. I was watching TV and they announced that Kennedy was shot. I dropped to my knees immediately asking God to spare his life. P.C., PARKERSBURG, WV

Like you, Abby, I was in Japan, a young NCO in a barracks thousands of miles from home. Home was New Jersey where my wife and family were.

I fell asleep with my radio on. When the stunning news came over the radio, I sat up in bed, unbelieving. I awoke some friends, and we all sat around in shock. When we went to the on-base snack bar, we met some Japanese workers who also were very "sorry about your president."

Through the grief for President Kennedy's family and for our nation, I thought, "We have come a long way from the time my dad, a marine, was fighting their dads on Iwo Jima." R.J.B., OMAHA, NE

I had been an honor guard in the White House under President Kennedy. On that day in 1963, I was on the U.S.S. *Wasp*. My buddies and I drove back from liberty in silence to be a part of the military guard along the funeral route. My uncanny resemblance to Lee Harvey Oswald elicited angry outbursts from many people, but I am proud to have known and served under President Kennedy. R.D.D., DALLAS, TX

Dear Abby . . .

I know where I was on 22 November 1963 (processing out of the air force), and I know where I will be on 22 November 1993. Living or not, I will be far away from any media. I liked, voted, honored, and mourned JFK; and I am thoroughly heartsick about the neverending road show, "Who killed Kennedy?" That media circus is enough to give paranoia a bad name. Let the man rest in peace! D.K., ST. PETERSBURG, FL

I t was a warm sunny day on the island of Okinawa. My husband announced that President Kennedy had been shot. I was terrified! There we were thousands of miles from home in one of the largest of our military installations in the Far East. I was sure that there was a conspiracy implicating the U.S.S.R. A declaration of war would naturally follow!

The island inhabitants were glued to their TV sets for days and the sad, glorious funeral was shown.
J.S., CLEARFIELD, UT

M y family was in Diyarbakir, Turkey, that fateful day. When our Turkish driver came to pick up my husband, he announced in halting English, "Your president is shot!" A beautiful memorial service was quickly planned and air force personnel openly wept. Ironically, the movie that had been scheduled to be shown that night was *PT-109*, the Kennedy war story.
J.H., ST. PETERSBURG, FL

. . . I Was in the Military

Yes, I know exactly where I was and what I was doing on 11–22–63! My husband and I, both stationed in Jacksonville, Florida, were given the afternoon off after the tragedy. Nine months later, our daughter was born in a very crowded maternity ward in Dallas, Texas. D.M., CLAYTON, CA

On November 22, 1963, I was in the U.S. Army stationed in Vinh Long, Mekong Delta, South Vietnam, assigned to the 114th Air Assault Company. Mr. Kennedy was not the only dear friend lost in that period of time. K.A.K., BELLEVILLE, IL

I was in a mine warfare training class at Ft. Belvoir, Virginia. I have never forgotten the callous reaction of a few southern fellow officer trainees who were delighted at the news. My own regret is that over that weekend I went home to NYC to family and friends rather than staying in D.C. to more personally witness the nations mourning. K.M.O., SEATTLE, WA

I was in Okinawa. After Kennedy was assassinated there was no leaving base, flags half-mast for one month, no social gatherings even in friends' homes (Thanksgiving just disappeared that

year), and only religious or very serious music on radio or in public.

Later in Taiwan, numbers of people bowed before us in the street and said, "We sorry your president die," long after the thirty day mourning period had passed.

A.P.G., KIRKLAND, WA

My husband was stationed in France. I first heard, "The president has been wounded," on Armed Forces Network. About twenty minutes later we learned the president had died. The base was on red alert. The army feared the U.S.S.R. would jump the Berlin Wall and try to speed across Germany during our disarray. The normally reticent French stopped me on the street of our little village to express their sympathy. The base had a memorial service. I held the wake as we gathered to listen to the funeral over the radio—Americans pulling together in a foreign land. J.T., JOPPA, MD

I was in the marines and was radio man for the company. I received a call from the regiment commander to call all the troops back to base immediately. Upon returning, we were packed up and went onto a DEFCON Four Alert Status. We were on trucks heading for the airbase at Camp Pendleton, California, with operational orders to invade Cuba, we assumed. The stand down came within hours. Even Vietnam never galvanized my emotions like that day. M.J., BOYCEVILLE, WI

My husband and I were in the Regina Hotel in downtown Kenitra, Morocco, North Africa. We had just arrived with our two children for a two-year stay with the U.S. Navy. One of the other tenants rapped on our door and told us she had just learned that JFK was dead. We were shocked. We spent the next three days explaining to the Moroccans that this was not a coup d'etat, and that the U.S. would go on as ever, sadly to be sure. F.G.D., FREEPORT, ME

I was working for the United States Air Force in Washington, D.C. When we heard that JFK had been killed, the wheels of government stopped. People were walking in a "coma," and crying and hugging each other. The newspapers printed EXTRAS. A friend and I went to Arlington Cemetery to say a prayer. We were there until sundown! J.G., PHOENIX, AZ

I was in basic training at Fort Gordon, Georgia. We had been in the field training, the day of Kennedy's death. In the evening a large formation was called

35

and it was announced that the president of the United States had been shot; our commander in chief was dead. We fellows were young and away from home for the first time; we thought our world had ended; we were positive that war would be next.

W.E.S., CANAL WINCHESTER, OH

I was a young man in the air force. We went on full alert. Didn't know if we might go into World War III. Scared to death! L.L., AUBURN, WA

My wife and I were watching To Kill a Mockingbird *in a Nigerian Army movie theater. Along with us were a black American woman and a Canadian man. The manager suddenly appeared in the dark near us and whispered hoarsely, "The president has been shot." We naturally assumed that he meant Nnamde Azikiwe, the Nigerian president. We thought of civil war. Would we be safe? But he corrected us: "No, no President* Kennedy! *President* Kennedy *has been shot!" We four, thousands of miles from home, stood under the light outside the*

*theater for hours, trying to make sense
of everything.*
   *For weeks afterward, strangers came
up to us on the street to ask, "Why did
you kill your president?" And you
know—every time, we felt somehow that
we* had.

D.M., RICHMOND, VA

On November 22, 1963, I was in a half-body cast in an army hospital after being involved in a helicopter crash not being able to move out of the hospital bed. Thinking that the Russians could invade us in a moment of confusion, the first thing they did was to issue me a rifle and live ammunition!

L.C.R., HILTON HEAD ISLAND, SC

My husband and I were stationed at an air force base near London, when we heard the terrible news. One of our neighbors, a lovely lady in her eighties, walked over in the bitter cold to express her condolences at 9:30 that evening. D.S.L., GOLDSBORO, NC

We were stationed in Waldorf, Germany. My daughter's sixty-five-year-old German piano teacher was giving her lessons when the news came on the radio. He sat still for a minute, then slowly got up, came to us and with tears streaming down his face said, "I cannot give lessons any more, my heart is broken." M.H., NORMAN, OK

I was at Ft. McClellan, Alabama, a private in the Women's Army Corps. We were in the middle of an exercise class, when a young second lieutenant, our instructor, suddenly called us to attention with tears in her eyes, and informed us our commander in chief had just been assassinated. I was very shocked yet at the same time very proud to have been serving my country at this time in history! C.H., OAKLAND, CA

I was a navy corpsman stationed at Bethesda Naval Hospital when news of President Kennedy's assassination was announced on the radio. All were in a state of disbelief. I was on the hospital grounds in front of the hospital when the body was brought there for autopsy. B.R., HAMPTON, VA

I was stationed at Williams Field with the U.S. Navy's "Operation Deepfreeze." After word was passed I went for a walk. With a strong wind blowing a "white out," I could see only a few feet ahead. In the middle of the compound was our American flag, standing out in the strong wind, at half-mast. It was then I realized it must be true, and broke out in tearful sobs as I stood there alone. The following days were torturous for us. We had only CB radio reports to cling to and missed seeing all the live TV coverage. M.M., HILO, HI

O ur family was living in Essex, England, because my father was in the air force. After the announcement, my dad had to leave immediately for the base—"Red Alert." We all lived in fear of "Red Alert" because we thought that meant a war would start. I remember crying and thinking we were all going to die. M.D., MINNEAPOLIS, MN

I was at Tachikawa Air Base in Japan. I got up early that Saturday morning and turned on the radio. They were saying that Vice-President Johnson had just taken the oath of office and President Kennedy had been taken to Parkland Hospital. We sat in shock. Who could ever forget that day—and all those to come. J.E.H., FT. WALTON BEACH, FL

I was in the U.S. Army stationed in Mannheim, Germany, in the Seventh Army Soldiers Chorus. We were practicing for a concert when we received the terrible news. We sat around stunned for

a while, and then one of the first tenors started to sing the spiritual, "Were You There When They Crucified My Lord?" There wasn't a dry eye in the rehearsal hall.

A.A., LINDENWOLD, NJ

Our family had just returned from my father's military funeral. The presentation of the flag "on behalf of the president of the United States" became much more special then because it was before the shooting. We recalled, too, how my father told us many times of his casual friendship with a younger John Kennedy during my father's twenty-two year navy career. C.V., ST. PETERSBURG, FL

I was a young airman. On the Monday morning following the assassination, there was a huge formation—the only one in my air force career. All personnel on the base stood at attention in a chilly drizzle listening to the general read General Orders No. 1 "Death of Commander in Chief." I still hear those drums. A.A.W., MENTONE, CA

4.

I Was Just a Child

DEAR ABBY: *My first memory is of JFK's assassination. I was watching a cartoon. My mom was ironing behind me. I became upset because the cartoon stopped and a man began talking. I changed channels and then Mom grabbed my hand and held me. She was crying. I forgot about the cartoon. I was confused and concerned about Mom. She tried to explain to me the best she could. I was almost three at the time.*

J.S., COLUMBIA, MO

On November 22, 1963, I was in my mother's lap crying. Why? Because *she* was. S.S., STILLWATER, OK

Because I was so young, and I knew that Texas was in the west, my first impression was that Kennedy and Oswald met in the town square and did the old "walk twenty paces, turn, and draw" routine. K.G., SYRACUSE, NY

I was paralyzed with fear that we would be bombed by the Russians since our president was dead. I believe I speak for many Americans who were just

42

children at that time when I say that we were a generation sincerely terrified of nuclear war. Air-raid drills were a routine part of every American classroom. I thank God that our children today do not have to fear. M.D.A., NUTLEY, NJ

When President Kennedy was shot, I was five years old, playing in our living room. The news came over the TV. My mother dropped to her knees and started crying. Still, to this day, this is one of my most vivid memories. D., WICHITA, KS

I was sitting at the kitchen table. The small black and white television was on. My mother was doing something at the kitchen counter. Her back was to the television. I do not remember what happened or what was said on television. I remember my mother holding on to the kitchen counter for support. I wasn't quite three-and-one-half years old.

D.B., BALTIMORE, MD

I was eight years old. I saved and still have the newspapers from that time. R.W., TACOMA, WA

I was about one month shy of being three years old. I heard my mom gasp, so I turned around. I saw the look on her face and I knew something of great significance had just occurred. I also remember her calling my dad at work right away to tell him the news. I think about that day often. S.B., LIBERTYVILLE, IL

I *was in one of the first Safeway Supermarkets in Salt Lake City with my mother when the announcement came over the loudspeaker. The lady in front of us dropped her groceries and fell to her knees. My mother had tears in her eyes. I looked up and asked her if that was Caroline's daddy, and my mother nodded yes. I remember feeling sad and not knowing exactly why.*

S.W.B., SALT LAKE CITY, UT

I was a little over two years old and I was wondering why cartoons were not on TV. My mom sat on the couch crying. I was afraid and confused. D.B., QUINLAN, TX

On November 22, 1963, I was eight years old and instead of being in school, my parents and I were in state court, suing the owner of a dog who bit me. When court was over, we saw about ten policemen huddled around a radio, listening to a report about the president having just been shot. ST. LOUIS, MO

My mother walked into the room after a telephone call from my dad. She said, "Your father just called. He's been shot." My first thought was that if he called, he's still alive. To this day, I remember my first reaction on hearing of President Kennedy's death was relief that it was him and not my dad.
K.M., LEWISVILLE, TX

Since I was the same age as Caroline, the president's daughter, I was always afraid that if I ever went to Dallas with my family, *my* father would be shot and killed. I carried that thought for years and even said it once in my second grade class. Everyone laughed. D.H., RINGWOOD, NJ

My grandmother, who was living with us then, was sitting on the sofa crying while the TV played. This shocked me because I had never seen an adult cry before. The newscaster announcing the president's death was also crying. G.D., LONG BEACH, CA

My mother tells me that as I stepped off the school bus I shouted to her, "Mommy, Mommy, they shot Lincoln." J.M., WHEAT RIDGE, CO

I was five years old. I do not know where I was on November 22, nor do I remember hearing of the assassination. But, I very *clearly* remember the funeral procession on TV. In the middle of the broadcast, my grandmother knelt by the sofa and had me join her as she prayed for our country. J.O., RIDGECREST, CA

When I got home from school the TV was on in the middle of the afternoon! My mother was in the kitchen fixing a pot of vegetable soup. I remember that as vividly as if it were yesterday, yet I remember nothing else about that day.

C.C., AUSTIN, TX

It was the first time I understood what it meant to die and the image of that television broadcast has been with me all my life. G.P., BURLINGTON, WA

We were watching "Bozo's Circus." During the grand prize game a very upset announcer interrupted the program with the grim news. I was too young to know who John F. Kennedy was, but I could tell from my mother's reaction he was somebody great and important. J.I., MT. PROSPECT, IL

This is my earliest childhood memory. My mother's soap opera was interrupted. This caused her momentary irritation at first—then the horrific news about President Kennedy. I can remember it so clearly—putting aside my red-and-white Romper Room calendar after my mother ran outside to share this tragedy with a close neighbor. A.V.S.N., JERICHO, NY

I confess that I do not have any recollection of the newscast. I do recall vividly, however, being told by a neighbor boy that, "The man who ran our country was shot by a crazy man, and now we have no president." Even at five years old, the enormity and sorrow of that day struck me enough to stay with me. L.B., MAYFIELD HEIGHTS, OH

My dad came home for lunch with tears running down his face. He said "Our president is dead." I was four years old. A.J.L., CHEROKEE, IA

I remember the televised funeral. I was upset that cartoons had been pre-empted. My aunt sat there and watched the procession with its riderless horse and little John John saluting his father, and she sobbed loudly the whole time. When I asked her why she was crying over someone she'd never met, she said, "It's such a shame—he was the best looking president we ever had." C.G., POWHATAN, VA

I was just two weeks away from my third birthday. I remember sitting in my diaper underneath the ironing board where my mother was ironing. She had the radio on and was listening to news reports of Kennedy's death. I remember looking up and seeing her grief-stricken face with tears flowing down it, and the wet tears sizzling as they hit the hot iron. This is my earliest childhood memory. S.G., OAKLAND, CA

I was three years old, sitting in my mother's lap. She began to cry while we watched TV. I told her to stop crying for the next three days. I personally remember the state funeral and to this day the sound of the drum cadence still echoes in my ears. M.B., BERKELEY, CA

I remember sitting in the black rocking chair in our family room, the sun spilling through the window. My mom sat perched on the edge of the sofa watching the television coverage as she methodically folded laundry into neat stacks, tears streaming down her face. D.M.M., SAN DIEGO, CA

. . . I Was Just a Child

I was a child, five years of age, when I heard of President Kennedy's assassination. I vividly remember the immense fear I felt any time I was in a crowd. I guess I felt that a sniper could be anywhere.

D.C., LONDONDERRY, OH

An older kid told us President Kennedy had been shot. I wasn't sure what that meant until I got home and found my mother crying in front of the TV. I had never seen her cry before. We watched TV for three days, and when I saw the horse with no rider, I cried too. M.M., CHITTENDEN, VT

I have two very distinct memories from my childhood: one, seeing my mother lying perfectly still in her coffin when I was five, and walking home early from the bus in 1963 because President Kennedy had been assassinated. I knew my life would be greatly altered. Every person is an important piece in the puzzle of life. I know having the one would have greatly helped me personally and the other, the country. N.K., HENSIOC, PA

I was only five years old, watching cartoons on our black and white TV in Fort Worth, Texas. An important news announcement brought my mother into our little living room. She listened for a moment, then covered her face and began to sob. "Mommy! What is it? Why are you crying?"

I still remember looking up at her, her face buried in her hands. "Someone has shot our president!" So I began to cry too, because she was so sad.

Years later, traveling abroad after high school, when foreigners learned I was from Texas they would say to me, "Oh, you killed Kennedy." I do believe that Texans carry around an eerie guilt about JFK's death. T.S., ROUND ROCK, TX

I remember pushing my doll in my doll carriage down the street where I lived in Brooklyn. I was on my way to visit my mother in the store where she worked. In my carriage, I had a portable radio and heard the president had been shot. I ran into the store to tell my mother. When I came outside my doll and radio had been stolen. I cried so hard. R.W., LIMA, NY

The day Kennedy was shot my family was moving into a new house. I was five years old and helped pick out the house. I remember hearing it on the radio, then watching the funeral on black and white TV. D.S., WELLSTON, OH

My mother picked me up from school in south Texas. It was a rainy, dreary day, just like in Dallas. Mom said the president had been shot; I said, "Murdered?" With that one word, a nine-year-old boy lost his innocence. M.M., NEW YORK, NY

I was four years old. It was the first "real" act of violence I had been exposed to. I wonder if a four-year-old today would remember such an event thirty years later.

S.J., TONEY, AL

5.

I Was Watching Television

DEAR ABBY: *As usual our three-month-old son was on top of the TV set, sleeping in a borrowed woven vegetable basket. (The warmth, music, voices, vibrations seemed to keep him contented.) The scene is still indelibly etched in vibrant Technicolor. Time does not fade a memory of trauma, especially when it invades one's living room.*

K.C., COON RAPIDS, MN

I was covering Styrofoam balls with velvet ribbon for Christmas ornaments to tie on packages. I was winding moss green velvet when the announcement came on TV. That ornament was not given away as the others were. It is always on our Christmas tree; we call it "The JFK." D.S.B., TALLMADGE, OH

I got the news that the president had been shot from TV's Walter Cronkite. I was in my living room with two young daughters and my eighty-year-old grand-mother. My husband was in the basement. I hollered the news down and he didn't believe me. We all cried. Our first son was born two months later. We named him John. P.V., ST. LOUIS, MO

Being ill on November 22, 1963, I was home watching Mike Douglas, a live TV talk show. When the station broke in with the horrible news, I went numb. All I remember was Mike Douglas telling his director, "How can I continue? How can I keep talking?" But he did continue, magnifying the stunned nation's emotions and expressing all of our questions and our grief. C.M., EUCLID, OH

I was standing at my kitchen sink doing dishes and all I had to do was to look to my right to the television set. I did and I froze. What a horrible, sick feeling. The *Challenger* crash comes to mind as an equal horror. R.H., PASCO, WA

I was lifting my neighbor's ill mother from where she was sitting to put her back to bed. She slumped in my arms and I said, "She's dead." The TV was on saying the president was shot. A double shock! T.S., MURRAY, UT

A home photographer took portraits of all three of my children that day. A half hour later, I was washing diapers and listening to "As the World Turns" when told. The portraits mark the moment.

A.C., BEAUMONT, CA

. . . I Was Watching Television

It was around noon. Our young son wandered into the kitchen to complain, "There are no cartoons on, just sad music." We hurried into the living room and sat in stunned silence as Walter Cronkite, with his voice breaking, told us JFK had been assassinated. The world has never been quite the same.
S.D.C., FALLS CITY, NE

I'm sixty-two years old now, but recall my six-year-old son rushing home from school two weeks prior to the assassination saying, "Mommy, Mommy the president has been shot!" I said, "No, it can't be. Let's turn on the TV and find out if it's true." No news concerning the president's welfare, so I tried to comfort him and convince him that no such tragedy had occurred.

Then two weeks later he rushed home with the same story. Once again I turned on the TV for proof, but this time, to my amazement, it was true. (My grandmother had ESP and my son was born on her birthday.) M.F., VALATIE, NY

I was sitting on my rocking chair watching my favorite soap and crocheting some yellow baby booties and hat, when the news came on TV. It was a very sad day indeed. I did not like the Kennedys, but it was a tragic thing that our president was killed.
M.S., JACKSONVILLE, FL

I was making turtle soup when the TV announced the assassination of President Kennedy. I never made turtle soup again, or ate it. T.H., BENICIA, CA

I was having a late lunch at Bookbinder's Restaurant in Philadelphia when one of the older, very distinguished black waiters ran to the corner of the large dining room to turn on the TV.

The first words we heard were, "President Kennedy has been shot in Dallas by a black man."

I have never seen people in such anguish as those waiters. At no time during the remainder of the broadcast or later did the network apologize or even mention the error of the irresponsible reporter.
F.W.O., HILLSBOROUGH, CA

I was visiting my daughter in Pomona, Missouri. I was helping her with her "mending and patching" when the news came over the TV of President Kennedy's death. Since we were Republicans there were no tears, but we were shocked!
L.M.R., WILLOW SPRING, MO

In 1963, I took a course in electronics and I had to build a TV from scratch. I finished it November 22.

When I turned it on the first news that came over the air was Jack Kennedy's assassination! T.A.P., SANDUSKY, OH

Where I was when I heard the news President Kennedy was shot was quite normal. I'm sure millions of other housewives were watching their soap operas. When the special announcement came on, I was very upset. The lasting effect it has had on me is to this very day when a special news announcement comes on, I think of President Kennedy and feel some sadness. J.R., YORK, PA

I was ill at home watching television. My mother-in-law who had emigrated from Russia in the early 1900s was there. She watched in complete silence and then said, "And now, darling, comes the Revolution." In view of the turmoil in our country these past thirty years, I am inclined to think she was right. Z.G.F., OMAHA, NE

I was waiting for the newspaper photographer to arrive to take our daughter's equestrian photo. Everything was ready so I turned on the TV and there was the tragic news. I didn't think the photo would be made that day, but he came anyway. Every time I come across this photo, I remember that sad day. T.S., ANDERSON, IN

I stopped my housework to prepare food for my infant son. I was holding him in my arms when the news came on TV. I remember thinking that President Kennedy was someone's little boy and I felt so much sorrow for the mother that held him and loved him.

I wondered what pain was ahead for my sweet baby boy. I've just learned to hope for the best, do the best I can as a parent, and try to deal with life's sorrows.

J.L., CLEARWATER, FL

Our church group was packing baskets of food to take to shut-ins for Thanksgiving when the news came on TV. L.A., AKRON, IA

On the day President Kennedy was shot I was in my daughters' bedroom. The youngest had had her tonsils out and we had moved the TV so she could watch it. I got very upset—much more upset than when either of my parents died. I had to leave the TV and go out to the kitchen for ice water and other things and later get supper for my husband and other three school kids. I was crying hard most of the time. B.F.H., ROCHESTER, NY

I was in Birmingham, Alabama, to get a divorce decree. I had just returned to my hotel room, turned on the TV to see

. . . I Was Watching Television

Jackie walking down the hospital hall-way by Jack's coffin. It was a doubly sad day for me.

L.E.

When President Kennedy was shot, I was in an underground storm shelter in our back yard. There were tornado warnings out. I came out to get the weather reports on the TV and heard the news. L.W., PINE BLUFF, AR

I was enjoying my quiet time while the children were napping. "As the World Turns" was interrupted by the news bulletin that the president had been shot. I gathered up the children and went to my neighbors. It wasn't a time to be alone. P.C.E., HOCKESSIN, DE

I was watching a TV news commentary while ironing when the program was abruptly interrupted by the news that the president had been shot. I felt completely paralyzed. Some thirty seconds later I realized I had not moved the iron—which had scorched a hole clear through the front of my husband's good

*dress shirt. He was not very happy
about it, but forgave me, considering
the circumstances.*

A.A.P., SHAKER HEIGHTS, OH

My mother and I were shopping at Northland
Center in Southfield, Michigan. A large crowd
had gathered in front of the entrance to the TV
department. The horror of the news of the assassination was multiplied at least fifty times as the same
scene and news were shown on every TV in the
department. D.W., ROYAL OAK, MI

I was watching TV when Walter Cronkite came on
and said that our President John Kennedy had been
shot. He was crying and I cried right along with him.
M.S., LAWTON, OK

I was watching "As the World Turns" when the
news flash broke in. I remember pulling our one-
year-old son onto my lap, sitting on a hassock in
front of the TV hugging him and crying and thinking,
"This is what it was like in 1865." G.K., LEXINGTON, OH

November 22, 1963, was our fifth anniversary. My
mother was visiting and I was taking advantage
of the children's naptime to make Christmas gifts for

neighbors—little pot-scrubbers from nylon net. The audio on the TV was low, but when the news came on, we turned it up.

We had dinner reservations, and we went. But the atmosphere was clouded with shock. E.H., BEVERLY HILLS, MI

It was a summer-like day and I was busy dressing my eighteen-month-old daughter to push her in her baby carriage to the park. All of a sudden it came on TV about President Kennedy being shot. I started crying and grabbed my daughter in my arms and ran to the door. The mailman was on the porch and I told him what had happened and we both were crying. My little girl said, "Mamma, why are you and Mr. Mailman so sad?" I told her we just lost our wonderful president. She still remembers that day too.
J.J.R., NORFOLK, VA

I was expecting a baby the last of November. When the TV program was interrupted with the news that President Kennedy had been shot, I started walking through the house praying and crying. I did that all day until I went into labor. My son, "Kennedy," was born at six that evening.

R.L.K., BESS, AL

6.

I Was in Dallas

DEAR ABBY: *On November 22, my three year old and I were driving to see the president arrive at lunch. As I approached the turn into Parkland Hospital, police sped up and stopped my car. The president's car sped in front of me. I drove in a few minutes later and a man with a press card in his hat and tears running down his cheeks told me the president was dead. It was another thirty minutes before the announcement was made. My son and I were almost alone as we watched history being made.*

J.K., CONROE, TX

On the day that President John Kennedy died, I was a tenth grader in a Spanish class at Bryan Adams High in Dallas. Everyone was aware of the president's visit. The principal spoke on the loud-speaker that our young president, my hero, had been killed. A hush came over the class and tears and sobs came from many students. My father was at the Trade Mart awaiting the president's arrival for a special dinner. Yes—I remember the day President Kennedy died. S., DALLAS, TX

Dear Abby . . .

I was in downtown Dallas about two blocks from where the president was shot. I was shopping with my sister, who was visiting from Los Angeles. We drove home in disbelief.

When *Robert* Kennedy was shot, I was visiting my sister in Los Angeles and was staying about two blocks from the Ambassador Hotel where the shooting took place. I was probably the only person alive who was that close to both of the shootings! I never did tell the news media as I was afraid someone would call me in to interrogate me. B.P., CEDAR HILL, TX

As a Dallas resident, I watched the parade down Main Street. The thing I remember most was Jacqueline Kennedy's bright pink hat and suit. After the entourage passed, I went to Sanger Bros. Department Store and someone said, "The president has been shot."

Soon after returning to my Oak Cliff suburb, where Lee Harvey Oswald also lived, I heard that he had been apprehended inside the Texas Theater. His seat was marked off as long as the theater was used. A.C., DALLAS, TX

I was in my room in the Dallas Hilton. I had just returned from watching the motorcade when I turned on the tube and heard Walter Cronkite say, "President Kennedy has been shot." What a disastrous day. W.D.L., ALBUQUERQUE, NM

I returned a rental car to the Dallas airport and boarded the next plane to Kansas City. As the plane was taxiing to its takeoff position, it was stopped so that the Kennedy party could come in for their landing (three planes). We saw the planes land and were all excited.

It was a beautiful clear morning in the Dallas area, but about fifteen minutes into the air we came into a weather change and clouds and rain made a very rough trip—bad weather all the way to Kansas City. On arrival we received the word but couldn't believe it. I suppose the pilots didn't want to upset the passengers. C.S., PRAIRIE VILLAGE, KS

I was working at the Veterans Administration Hospital and my daughter was an X-ray technician at Parkland Hospital. At the VA Hospital you could have heard a pin drop throughout that nine story building. I don't care what political party you belonged to, the tears flowed freely and unashamedly from everyone's eyes. D.G.S., TRINIDAD, CO

I had left my job as leader of a trio band in a local club, but was still writing music for some people. A day or two after the assassination my wife called me and told me Oswald had been shot, and my former boss, Jack Ruby, was suspected. I visited him in jail and he

Dear Abby . . .

showed no remorse. I have a copy of the last contract we signed for the services of the trio. F.H.F., BIRMINGHAM, AL

I t was during my junior year at SMU. The city of Dallas literally shut down. Lights were out, no one was on the street, people were in shock and deep grief. I remember receiving from my parents in New Jersey a front page from one of the papers indicating that Texans had killed the president. That was so far from the truth. He had been welcomed as a great person, and most Texans were devastated.

D.E.H., ROCKWELL, NC

I was living in Dallas, but was in Manhattan on business the day of the assassination. That night a restaurant owner ordered me out of his cafe upon learning I was from Dallas. I have never been back to New York. G.F.F., DALLAS, TX

W e were on our honeymoon, going through Dallas. We saw Kennedy's plane circle the airport prior to landing. We were tuned to the radio as we pro-

66

ceeded through Dallas. Static was bad so we turned off the radio. As we began leaving the main part of the city, we turned on the radio only to hear screaming that JFK had been shot. Our hearts sank, and from then on we were glued to the radio until we reached our home in Michigan. M.A.S., GARDEN CITY, MI

My son and I were watching the presidential motorcade in Dallas. We watched when President Kennedy was shot and Mrs. Kennedy was crawling over the back seat panic-stricken. A traumatic experience knowing this was for real. That day made an indelible mark on our memory. It seems like yesterday and it has been thirty years. Thank you for asking this of us. M.B.B., ALBUQUERQUE, NM

Early on November 22, 1963, I was excused from my job at the Corps of Engineers in Fort Worth, Texas, to step outside onto the street to see President and Mrs. Kennedy drive by in their limousine from their hotel on their scheduled trip to Dallas.

As the president turned to face my side of the street where I stood alone, he answered my wave with his.

67

Dear Abby . . .

> *An hour later, as I was describing that scene to my fellow workers, the news of the shooting came over the air. What a memory!*

E.P., WOODLANDS, TX

On that fateful day I was working in downtown Dallas. My office mates and I had just returned to our office from seeing the president and Jackie, when we heard the sirens and then the terrible news. To this day, I hate to hear sirens since they went on for hours that day. I was close enough to see his penetrating blue eyes and her lovely pink suit. J.R., ANNAPOLIS, MD

I was on the fourth floor of the Terminal Annex Post Office and had just turned from the window after watching President Kennedy's motorcade turn in front of the Texas School Book Depository when someone said, "There's been a shot!" I turned just in time to see the Secret Service men jump on the president's car and the car speed forward en route to Parkland Hospital. It was an unobstructed view and one I will never forget. Police were going in all directions, especially up the hill toward the railroad tracks. Also there was a man spread out on the grass with a child under each arm. It was a day I will remember as long as I live. S.T.P., DALLAS, TX

Seven girls and I skipped school to see the president. We were at the front of the crowd when the car came by and I touched the side of it as it passed.

Twenty minutes later, we were watching a movie at the Palace Theater when they announced first, he'd been shot, and then he was dead. A piano rose from the orchestra pit and played the "Star-Spangled Banner." S.F., COSTA MESA, CA

I was there. I saw the president. I heard the shots. No one will ever convince me there were not four shots fired. I thought they were fireworks!

R.M., KELLAR, TX

When Kennedy was shot, I was at Parkland—a student nurse. I heard all the department chiefs being paged. I saw all the press buses arriving; watched the E.R. grow crowded; saw Jackie in her bloodstained pink suit. Thirty years later, I find it hard to believe I was there. J.D., SAN ANGELO, TX

As the manager of an airline catering facility at Love Field, I was acutely aware of the intense grief and feeling of insufficiency engendered by this base act. Activity at this major airport almost stopped for the period between 1:00 and 2:00 p.m. People moved as in a daze, overwhelmed by the enormity of this cowardly act. I saw Air Force One started and running for more than two hours; limos arrived and departed discharging and picking up people. Finally, just before 3:00 p.m., Air Force One lifted off for the return to Washington. D.M.C., LLANO, TX

I was at Love Field. I had been running a TV camera showing the arrival of the president and his wife. When they left, I went into the terminal to relax, and the first thing I knew, I was being questioned by the FBI. When I showed my TV credentials they told me that Kennedy had been shot. I was at Parkland Hospital when they announced his death. I took pictures of the policeman's funeral and Lee Harvey Oswald. S.D., POTTSBORO, TX

Four of us took the morning off (with our parents' permission) from our sophomore year at Dallas High School and went to Love Field to wait for the president's plane to land. While eating breakfast, a small plane on fire came in, and we all decided that was the most exciting thing we'd see that day. We watched the motorcade at Lee Park, and the President and Mrs. Kennedy were just over an arm's length away. I've never forgotten how gray his hair was. After the motorcade passed, we headed back to

school. We heard the announcement on the car radio and went back to my house where we spent the rest of the next three days glued to the television. Kennedy was buried on my seventeenth birthday.
N.R., BEDFORD, TX

As soon as the president's and vice-president's limousines passed by, we headed back to the office and had walked about two blocks when Dallas became a solid shrill of sirens with police cars going in all directions. A feeling that words cannot describe, and the sound of sirens that I can hear till this day. M.K., NAPLES, TX

On November 22, 1963, I was assigned the honor of being the installer in charge of attaching the telephone communications lines in Air Force One when it arrived in Dallas. After I finished, the Secret Service men took my partner and me over next to the president's limousine while he was greeting the crowd. He came to the car and looked up at us and smiled. Little did I know what was to happen to him just thirty minutes later. W.E.F., PIPE CREEK, TX

Friday, November 22, 1963, was our wedding day. We were having a family luncheon when the restaurant owner announced that President Kennedy had been shot.

We married that evening in Denton, Texas, just thirty-five miles north of Dallas. We spent the first night of our honeymoon in Dallas. The city was like a tomb. Every anniversary is a painful reminder of that fateful day. J.& R.G., HENRIETTA, TX

I was at Love Field and shook hands with Kennedy and Jackie as their open-topped car stopped right next to me. I have close-up photos better than any reporter took. On the way home we heard on the car radio that he had been shot.

A.M.M., DALLAS, TX

I was just barely eight years old at the time, but there is no other day in my childhood that is as memorable. I was in St. Thomas Aquinas Grade School. The principal announced that Kennedy had been shot, and she began to lead us in praying the rosary. He died before we finished. I remember how her voice trailed off as she uttered the words. P.M., DALLAS, TX

I was working at a doctor's answering service when we got the report. In a few minutes I left the telephone and went to the radio where I called the doctors by radio to go to Parkland Hospital to care for Kennedy! R.W., ARLINGTON, TX

I was at the parade about four blocks from the school book depository. I could have touched him.

I didn't know then that this event would cause some excitement in my life. Since 1963 I have been in three movies that have re-created the parade. I played Lyndon Johnson in *The Trial of Lee Harvey Oswald*, *JFK*, and *Ruby*. B.E., DALLAS, TX

On November 22, 1963, I drove by the Dallas Trade Mart as President Kennedy came out. We waved as he got in his auto for his last and fatal auto ride. J.R.B., HOUSTON, TX

I was a Red Cross volunteer at Parkland Hospital when President Kennedy died there. A plainclothes policeman asked me to bring coffee which was given to L.B.J. and Lady Bird. We were all in a state of shock and will never forget it.

A.S., DALLAS, TX

I was standing on the corner of Lemmon Avenue and Turtle Creek Boulevard, headed for downtown Dallas. I was so close. I was amazed at his coloring, because I had only seen him previously on black and white TV. He was very fair, almost pink, and his hair was almost blonde in the sunlight.

I was so excited that I wanted to see him again so I headed for Market Hall. The president's car made the exit going maybe 70 mph, and a black tarp was covering the back. I knew immediately something was wrong. Nothing in my life had prepared me for this. I cried. P.N.M., DALLAS, TX

7.

I Was in School

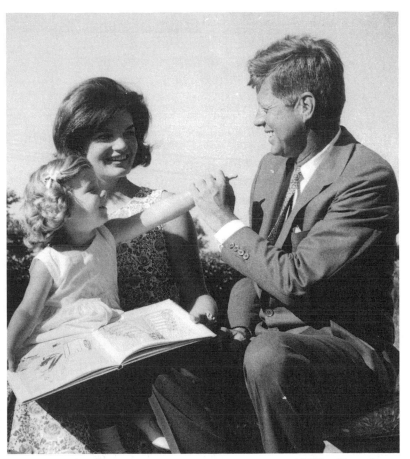

DEAR ABBY: *The news broke for me while in my sophomore gym class. The coach sat in his office just staring at his radio until almost twenty minutes after normal starting time. He then just got up, walked into the gym, and stood very still for about a minute staring into space. Then without warning he spun around and hurled a baseball at the wall so hard the cover split off the ball and several large chips broke off the brick wall. Then he started to cry openly and said, "Some God-damned bastard just killed the president." I don't know what shocked us more—the news or the fact that this soft-spoken man who had suspended students for swearing had sworn so violently and openly in front of us. He went back into the office and sat at his desk—weeping.*

M.D.B., FRANKENTHAL, GERMANY

A coed from India ran into the room and said, "The president's been shot." My world was so small I thought it was the university president. R.M.F., WHEELING, WV

. . . *I Was in School*

I was going to college in D.C. when President Kennedy was shot. My roommate and I went to the White House where we saw the day suddenly turn grey with hundreds of government employees pouring out of the buildings with many falling to their knees in tears. On the White House lawn a helicopter came for Caroline and John John. An incredible moment.

S.S., LACOSTA, CA

Our teacher said, "You will never forget this day nor what you were doing." I never have.

L., KENNEBUNK, ME

I was in third grade in a Catholic school when the news came over the loudspeaker. The sister cried, then we were all sent home. At that age I thought that was the way we got rid of our presidents. Later when I saw Mrs. Kennedy on TV moving out of the White House so Mrs. Johnson could move in, I thought, "The least they could do for Mrs. Kennedy was to let her keep the house."

P.J.S., LOS ANGELES, CA

77

I was in second grade. When the nuns learned of the assassination, they herded all of us into the basement, convinced that the bombs would start falling at any minute. T.O., NEW YORK, NY

I was in my sixth grade class drawing a picture of John Kennedy and Abe Lincoln standing on a cloud looking down on people. Someone asked why Kennedy was on the cloud as he was not dead. Then the announcement came that the president was shot. I felt horrible—like I was responsible. K.R., COLUMBUS, OH

When JFK was shot, I was an eighteen-year-old Rotary Exchange Student living in Soderhamn, Sweden. The next morning my classmates excitedly crowded around me. "Had I heard the news?" I had. "Was I of the same political party as Kennedy?" No. "Was I happy or sad about his death?" Sad. Their expressions changed instantly from curious and excited to sympathetic and understanding. They had learned something about America.

E.P.K., NEW KENSINGTON, PA

I had just turned thirteen years old and was in seventh grade. We were informed that the president was dead, ordered to put our heads on our desks, and to close our eyes. We were sent home shortly thereafter.

When my dad walked in, we all rushed up to him, including my mother, and told him that the president had been shot and killed. He dropped his metal lunch bucket on the living room floor and started to tremble. He did not know! He worked for the federal government and he did not know!

My dad quickly regained his composure, but I will never forget that moment because it was the one and only time I ever saw him show any emotion.

M.K., HOLT, MO

B ack in those days there was no "grief counseling" offered, but I was lucky because I had one very caring teacher who talked and let us talk about it.

K.F., ST. PETERSBURG, FL

I will never forget November 22, 1963. I was a seventh grader, sitting in my home room class when a neighboring teacher came to ask to borrow our TV. She indicated that the president had just been shot! We were shocked, and turned to our teacher, assuming we would be allowed to watch the newscast also. I will never forget her response: "No, we need to read our Weekly Readers." After thirty years, I am still dumbfounded at that response.

L.K.W., LIBERTY, MO

> **M**y third grade class stood in front of the stage waiting to purchase afternoon milk. I vividly remember wearing a burgundy cotton dress with covered buttons and a Peter Pan collar, as well as holding three pennies for milk.
>
> L.A., SPRINGFIELD, MO

I was in kindergarten in Grand Island, Nebraska. When I got home my mom was crying. The funeral was on television and people everywhere were upset, and there was only one page left on the calendar. I was terrified. I thought the world was ending. I was so relieved when my mom put up a new calendar, and explained all the madness. P.A., BELLEVILLE, IL

I was a sophomore in high school, and I was in study hall reading *The Day Lincoln Was Shot.* Surreal, huh?! K.S., VAN WERT, OH

. . . I Was in School

I was in the seventh grade. My teacher told us that President Kennedy was shot. He then asked, "Who will be president if Kennedy dies?" No one knew the answer. Our homework assignment that night was to write *"Lyndon Baines Johnson"* five hundred times! I'll never forget it! S.G.R., QUINCY, MA

I was in the sixth grade in a Maryland suburb. My mother took my sister and me to watch the funeral procession because she hoped we would never have such an opportunity again.

So do I! His death shocked me, but I reacted much more emotionally when Bobby Kennedy was assassinated. The year 1963 was a sad time, but as a much more aware high school student, I thought 1968 was the absolute nadir since we lost a spiritual leader (Dr. King) and a political leader (RFK).

K.F.H., SANTA CLARITA, CA

I was a flag monitor in sixth grade. Another girl and I were sent out to lower the flag before going home because our president had been killed.
P.W., LOS ANGELES, CA

I was in fifth grade, and less than three hours earlier, our school had bused all the students to line Highway 183 to watch his motorcade pass. President Kennedy had spent his last night on earth in my hometown—then it was on to Carswell Air Force Base and Dallas.

I remember hearing the principal's voice coming over the intercom announcing President Kennedy's death. I remember saying out loud, "NO!! We just saw him. He can't be dead!" I remember his smile, and Jackie's pink suit. That day is forever etched in my mind. Too bad there weren't counselors in those days. We needed one! S.G., FORT WORTH, TX

I was playing on the school grounds when I heard about the assassination of President Kennedy. There was a terrible panic among my friends and me. We thought the whole world was coming to an end, and the Russians were going to come to the United States and start a war. N.F., WALNUT CREEK, CA

November 22, 1963. Southern Methodist University, Dallas. Got to Mustang Band practice at 1:00. Heard news of death on transistor radio. Radio thrown to ground. Tears. Shock. Horror. Fear. Lost faces seen that night at Dealy Plaza. More gun shots. Oswald dead. News learned during worship at Perkins Chapel, SMU. The world has never been the same since. J.D., NORTH LITTLE ROCK, AR

. . . I Was in School

I came from a strong, active Republican family and had a friend from a strong, active Democratic family. I was in seventh grade and the person who told me about the assassination was my Democratic friend. I am ashamed to admit my comment was, "Good." I then realized Johnson would be president and commented, "Oh no, that means Johnson will be president. He's even worse."

I've been ashamed of my comments for thirty years and don't tell people what I said. I want parents to realize that their reasonable and honest convictions can so easily be distorted by their kids. It actually took my humanity away. Although we may prefer one politician over another, all are people, just with differing opinions on how to serve their country. ELKHORN, WI

I was returning from lunch at Bishop Noll High School. Word spread through the crowd and I remember wondering *how* President Kennedy could have been shot because he wasn't a hunter. Assassination *never* crossed my mind. C.J.M. (APO POSTMARK)

I was a senior in high school. It wasn't until fifth period that the thought hit me, that this would be the perfect time for the Russians to attack us. I was convinced we would be bombed! I even

heard teachers talking about "evacuation routes."

It seems we sat and stared at the TV for days on end. I think the picture of little John John saluting his father's casket is one we all remember, but another one that I still see so clearly was taken at the place where the president was to speak that day. A black man who was a waiter was leaning on a table with a towel over his arm and a serving tray in his hand. His other hand covered his eyes, as his shoulders shook and tears ran down his face.

J.C., TACOMA, WA

I remember getting off the school bus, and seeing the fire station on my corner had already been draped in black with the flag at half-staff.

R.H.P., E. BRIDGEWATER, MA

I was in a third grade spelling bee. After hearing the shocking news, the smartest girl in our class received her next word—short. She promptly spelled it S-H-O-T. S.V., LINCOLN, NE

. . . I Was in School

I was seventeen and a senior in high school. I was coming out of gym class heading toward Social Studies when I saw the flag being lowered to half-mast. Then a moment of silence was called and the announcement was made that President Kennedy had been shot. My Social Studies teacher had been in the service with President Kennedy. He smashed his eyeglasses against the wall, and cried with the students. I had buried my mother on November 16, and felt doubly grieved. N.M., GOLDEN, CO

I was in first grade class at Highland Elementary School in New Castle, Pennsylvania. When we returned from Christmas vacation in January 1964, our school had been renamed "The John F. Kennedy Elementary School." M.P., SHERMAN OAKS, CA

I was a freshman student at Marymount College in Arlington, Virginia. Because of our proximity to Washington, D.C., the phone service went dead for several hours. No calls in or out. We got all our news by radio or TV.

I was at the White House when Jackie Kennedy's helicopter landed. She was still in her pink suit, covered with blood.

I also witnessed the funeral—standing along the avenue as the family, riderless horse, and dignitaries passed. It was a sad, horrible time. P.C.V., SAN JOSE, CA

Dear Abby . . .

I had gone to New York City for the day to visit the secretarial school I planned to attend. As I made my way through the streets of Manhattan, I heard church bells ringing in the early afternoon but paid no heed—I was too busy trying to find my destination. Later, on the subway, I saw people crying but still didn't think anything was wrong. Finally, walking back to my car, a delivery truck passed by and threw out "extra" editions of the *New York Daily News.* Imagine my shock when I read that my beloved president, JFK, was dead. E.S., BAYVILLE, NJ

I was in St. Augustine School in Hartford, Connecticut, in the seventh grade with Sister John Francis. Sister Lucy announced JFK's death. I was only thirteen, but what really freaked me out was to discover that *nuns* could cry. I never thought of them that way. F.B., ALBUQUERQUE, NM

Walking home from school, a big bully had us all in tears because he said that the whites would round up all the coloreds and hang us "KKK style." A significant emotional event for a twelve year old! L.W., UPLAND, CA

A high school sophomore, I was in gym. After we were told, the locker

*room got so quiet. I overheard an older
girl saying, "Look, even Miss Feinberg
is crying, and she's a Jew." I was only
fifteen and those were more naive times;
I didn't see what ethnic heritage had to
do with grief. Thirty years later, I still
don't.*

K.W., PETALUMA, CA

We were dismissed from school early that day, and I walked home frightened and confused. I found my mother and my teenaged cousin, with mascara-streaked face, sitting very close to the TV watching the coverage of the assassination. I joined them, finding the coverage lurid but compelling. I was afraid to watch, and afraid not to watch. J.D., LITTLE CANADA, MN

As a student at the University of Oregon, probably one hundred students sat in stunned silence as the voice gave a moment by moment account of the shooting in Dallas. It felt like nothing would ever be the same. Homecoming was to have been that weekend. It was canceled. I can't even remember if it was ever rescheduled. I guess it was, but it didn't matter because dreams were canceled that day—forever.

J.S., THOUSAND OAKS, CA

Dear Abby . . .

I was in sixth grade and I heard the announcer say, "The president is dead of his bullet wounds." I had never heard that phrase "dead of" before, and while I was contemplating its meaning, our teacher started to cry. L.H., PORTLAND, OR

A s a class of ten-year-olds we did not know what "assassination" meant because it was not a familiar word to us then. By 1968, the word would become unfortunately an all too common one.
W.F.S., FRESH MEADOWS, NY

A fter school, I ran home and remembering my parents voted for Nixon I said, "Mommy, does this mean the man you voted for can be president now?"

S.B., MORGAN CITY, LA

I was a freshman at Mary Washington College in Fredericksburg, Virginia. Walking back to the dorm, there was such a deathly hush—I remember wondering how all those old stone buildings could remain standing after what had happened. I fully expected the world to stop spinning. C.F.C., RICHMOND, VA

I was in fifth grade homeroom in Red Bank, Tennessee. Becky shouted, "Someone killed Kennedy!" About half the class stood up and cheered. My teacher quickly rebuked the class with, "I don't care how you feel about the man, but show some respect for the office." K.R.C., AUSTIN, TX

I was a sophomore in college totally engrossed in myself. As I look back, I feel this moment in time was the beginning of my growing up. So many things changed that day. For the first time in my life, I was more concerned about my country, our president, the world situation, politics, wars, peace, and loyalty rather than the rival football game on Saturday, the Kappa party on Friday night, or if Roger was really going to ask me to Homecoming. B.B.G., LONGVIEW, TX

It was just prior to our weekly pep rally. The principal solemnly walked to the podium and asked us to rise and sing the National Anthem. There were no partisan feelings in the gym that day, just grieving students who couldn't comprehend the death of a president at the hands of an assassin.

S.K., ALLENTOWN, PA

I was in my second grade class. After the announcement came over the loudspeaker, we were asked to bow our heads to say a prayer for him (it was allowed back then). Even at that early age I felt the grief and realized what a tragedy it was.

N.M., BERCHTESGADEN, GERMANY

That moment forever changed my outlook and the "sixties" started. Not the Beatles or the Stones, but President Kennedy's death started it.

C.O., RICHMOND, VA

8.
I Was Abroad

Dear Abby . . .

DEAR ABBY: *We were living in Karachi, Pakistan. That day, which in Pakistan was the morning of November 23, we had gone to the open market as usual. As we entered, the vendors left their stalls and rushed toward us crying, "Sahib! Memsahib! Your king is dead! Your king is dead!" We didn't understand their meaning until one Pakistani said, "Kennedy." At first we thought he was talking about the elderly Kennedy, who had been so ill. But the Pakistanis were so distraught that we soon realized that they were telling us something much more terrible—that it was our beloved President John F. Kennedy, our "king," who had died.*

R.M. & H.W., OAKLAND, CA

It was my first time traveling with a professional dance troupe in San Jose, Costa Rica, and the first time out of the States. We were rehearsing on the top floor of the Balmoral Hotel. It was very frightening. I kept hoping it wasn't true—a very lonely feeling being away from home and then not being able to understand the news in Spanish. J.L.D., IOWA CITY, IA

Returning from our honeymoon in England, disbelief then shock prevailed. The security at Logan Airport was not to be believed. Britain stopped also! S.A.S., SOUTH EASTON, MA

My family and I were living in Santa Cruz, Bolivia. There were no TV, no telephones, and no newspapers. The Gulf Oil Company received the message. The news spread and everyone was crying, including the Bolivians. All businesses closed for three days and black ribbon bows were placed at the doors. The Bolivian people loved Kennedy because he was Catholic and he was helping Bolivia with the Point Four Program and Peace Corps. C.A., EL PASO, TX

We were living in Ankara, Turkey, on November 22, 1963. It was as if the sky had fallen. The American and Turkish citizens were very sad. All the embassies flew their flags at half-staff to honor our fallen president. There was a day of complete silence in the whole city of Ankara. R.J.B., BEREA, OH

My wife and I were in Amsterdam. The hotel manager brought us the news of Kennedy's assassination and expressed his and the staff's great

*sorrow. The hotel saw that we had
English newspapers and TV coverage
from the U.S. We were also taken to the
U.S. Embassy to register our condolences.
The city turned off all holiday lights,
canceled all events, and displayed President Kennedy's draped picture in every
store window and building lobby. A huge
memorial was held at Dams square—
over one hundred thousand attended. The
people were fearful that World War III
would start in Europe and that the U.S.
government would collapse.*

L.A.W., LA MARQUE, TX

I was in the Peace Corps in Liberia, West Africa,
when the tragic news came over the short-wave
radio on the "Voice of America." I will always remember the deep sorrow expressed by the people of
Liberia over the death of the man who inspired me to
join the Peace Corps. R.H., LOS ANGELES, CA

*I was working in West Berlin. Within a
half hour of the news flash, the Hilton
had darkened every room facing toward*

*the downtown area of the city, and put
a single burning candle on each window
sill. Soon in nearly every window up
and down all of the streets, all that
could be seen was a single candle burning in each darkened window. I have
never seen or experienced such an outpouring of emotion from so many people
in such a few short minutes.*

D.E.S., SILVERTON, OR

On November 22, 1963, my wife and I were in
Saigon, South Vietnam, where I was a U.S. government employee. I heard the news of President
John F. Kennedy's assassination on the radio. I rushed
to the kitchen to tell my wife, and she explained to
the Vietnamese maid that a man had just shot the
president of the United States.

The maid, who knew little about America, asked,
"Why did he shoot him? Did he want to be president?" F.T., TAUNTON, MA

I was vacationing in India and had gotten up early to
see the Taj Mahal at sunrise. An Indian gentleman
came up to me and said, "I am so sorry about your
president." I could hardly believe it at first, but was

to hear those same words from many strangers
of many nationalities during the rest of the trip.
D.L., HAYWARD, CA

I was an eighteen year old growing up in Finland.
I was listening to the radio when a news bulletin
broke in. The color was gone from my mom's face
and she gasped, "The Russians must be coming."
T.S., PASADENA, CA

I was in Moscow. As I entered my hotel, the "Voice
of America" was speaking about President Johnson.
Then the awful news! What isolation and desolation we
American educators felt so far from home.

Later, in the hotel dining room, our Russian
waiters wept with us. In spite of the Cold War, we
found kinship on that dark night. W.T., DOVER, DE

*My mother and I were at a concert at
Robert College in Istanbul, Turkey,
when we learned that President Kennedy
had been shot. Our Turkish friends and
associates treated us as though we had
lost a member of our immediate family.
Flags were flown at half-mast for three
days and only classical music was*

*played on Turkish radio for thirty days.
I believe it was the first time in the
history of Turkey that there was public
mourning for a foreigner.*

R.D.H., APEX, NC

I was a six year old living in Havana, Cuba. I will
always recall the Missile Crisis as a time of terror.
Then, on the afternoon of November 22, everything
was too quiet in the house! As dusk fell, my family
tuned into the "Voice of America" (listening to it was
a crime) in the dark and heard that President Kennedy had been assassinated. On my aunt's face, there
was a final look of resignation, as if all were lost. I
will always remember listening to the radio and night
falling on a room we were too frightened to light.
M.H., DUNEDIN, FL

I got news of Kennedy's death sitting in a remote
airport near Puerto Cabezas on Nicaragua's east
coast. The whole country went into mourning. It was
two days before banks, stores, etc. went back to
work. In Managua there was a mock state funeral
held at the big Catholic church. People consoled us
there also. T.H., VENTURA, CA

I was in the Vienna Opera at a performance of Wagner's Die Walkure. *In the final scene, the god Wotan raised his spear and, to the majestic chords of the Magic Fire Music, the flames leapt up and slowly surrounded the sleeping Brunhilde, and the final curtain came down. Before the audience could applaud, an official stepped quickly out onto the stage. "Ladies and gentlemen," he announced, "it saddens me to inform you that John F. Kennedy, president of the United States, is dead."*

There was no applause that night. The audience hurried mutely from the theater. Outside the newspaper vendors were swamped. When I reached one of them, disbelief piled on top of shock and incomprehension: Fiel einem Attentat zum Opfer, *read the headline—Victim of Assassination.*

P.A.M., OREGON CITY, OR

We were all at the Imperial Hotel in Tokyo when some Americans we had met telephoned us from the lobby and gave us the news. We joined them

downstairs and wept openly with Americans. The
Japanese, reputed to be unemotional, wept with us.
JFK was loved by them and still is. J.& E., NEW YORK, NY

My sister, her husband, and I were in
Sweden. We heard the news on the
radio, in Swedish. The next day and
until the burial everything was closed—
all theaters, entertainment of all kinds,
and many other stores. In every window
of the homes and apartment buildings
were the American and Swedish flags
and candles. Very moving.

I gave several piano concerts after this
time and played a number in memory
of our president—Du Bist Die Ruh.
Every time I began to play it, the entire
audience stood up. Another moving in-
cident. I wrote to Jacqueline Kennedy
and received a nice reply.

A.D.L., MINNEAPOLIS, MN

On November 22, 1963, I was in the Peace Corps
in Nepal, South Asia. A tearful, out of breath student ran all the way to school to tell me my "boss
was killed." M.V., NAPERVILLE, IL

Dear Abby . . .

My husband, myself, and two children lived in an oil camp in an isolated area of southern Iran far from civilization. In the local bazaar, radios were blaring something in Farsi which we did not understand. Sensing that something was wrong by the looks the locals were giving us, we returned to camp and dug out the short-wave radio. The Russians had lifted their jamming of the "Voice of America," and we heard the terrible news. J.W., IRVINE, CA

My husband and I were in Barcelona, Spain, on November 22, 1963. The concierge of our hotel told us our president had been assassinated. The impact of his news prompted us to go outside. There was not a newspaper to buy, and as we walked we were approached by many people expressing their sympathy to us. I don't think we ever had dinner that night.

The next morning the elevator operator said police had captured the killer, but someone murdered him in the police station. He then said, "What's wrong with you Americans? Are you all crazy?" With the news we were receiving it seemed very likely.

M.S.M., ST. LOUIS, MO

We were deep in the interior on New Guinea, listening to our short-wave battery operated radio. An announcement came over declaring the assassination. First reaction: tragic! Next, what is happening to America that such a senseless act could take place. We vividly remember this tragedy. G. & M.H., VERO BEACH, FL

I was in London attending a ballet starring Dame Margot Fonteyn and Rudolf Nureyev when the manager interrupted the performance to say, "England has lost one of her greatest friends, President Kennedy was assassinated." Flags were flown at half-mast, and for days afterward, strangers stopped me on the street to express sympathy.

E.G.B., SAN FRANCISCO, CA

My husband, three small sons, and I had just arrived in Dhahran, Saudi Arabia. We heard the news in the company commissary. Needless to say, everyone in camp was upset and the local Saudis could not understand why we did not execute the assassin right away. D.R., SPRINGFIELD, PA

I was living in Rome, Italy, working on the *Daily American* newspaper. As I kept my eyes on the wire service machine, "Kennedy dead" came out. I wouldn't tell anyone. I felt as long as I didn't say it, it wouldn't be true. I prayed for a retraction. None came—the tape kept repeating that terrible line. I finally gave it to a reporter. A dreadful day.

A.C.S., MERRITT ISLAND, FL

Iwas a sophomore in history class in a private girls school in Sri Lanka. I had to leave school that day because I was so upset. I wrote a sympathy letter to Jackie and she responded. I regret that the letter was misplaced in my move here twenty-five years ago.

S.C., TRUMBULL, CT

We lived in Belfast, Northern Ireland, the only Americans living in the Holywood area. Within hours strangers began ringing our doorbell expressing their sympathy. The following day no one passed without pausing to shake my hand or say a few words. The Irish kindness and sincere friendship was a very touching unforgettable experience. J.E., PORT CHARLOTTE, FL

My husband and I were vacationing in Acapulco, Mexico, on November

22, 1963. That evening we sat with other Americans in the hotel lobby watching TV news. Everyone was sympathetic and emotionally upset. The border was closed for a few hours which was frightening.

But, the good news is that nine months later we had a fine baby boy. We named him John.

H.W.E., FLORENCE, SC

We were living in a small town, Welford, England. My neighbor's twin daughters came to the door all excited and said, "Mum said turn on the telly. Your Prime Minister has been shot!" The news shocked me beyond words and I longed to be back home. It's a time in history I shall never forget.

H.B.L., BRICKTOWN, NJ

When President Kennedy was shot, I was working in the U.S. Embassy in La Paz, Bolivia. I was in shock being so far from home. All the news was in Spanish which was frustrating since I spoke so little Spanish. The Bolivian people really felt our sorrow.

D.L., PORTLAND, OR

Dear Abby . . .

On that day just before Thanksgiving, I was in Scotland as a computer consultant. When I made my usual entrance into the pub, to my surprise every person stood up in utter silence. After a few moments an Englishman stepped forward and said, "Yank, do you know that your president was assassinated this afternoon?"

The European reaction to his death was extraordinary. From that moment on, as long as I stayed in that hotel, I could not buy a drink in the pub. To all the Scots, Brits, and Europeans there, I represented the only available American to whom they could express their sorrow. It was a dramatic experience which brought to my attention how much the world loved John F. Kennedy.

R.N., EAGLE LAKE, FL

I was having dinner in a London restaurant with two fellow Peace Corps volunteers when we learned President Kennedy had been shot. We were overcome because we were returning home from two years in Thailand as members of the first "pioneering" group of Peace Corps volunteers to Thailand in response to "ask not what your country. . ." J.K., FRAMINGHAM, MA

We were in Peshawar, West Pakistan, the day JFK was killed. Scarcely had our consul informed us, when our neighbors and my SEATO husband's students and colleagues came to call, console, and bring food gifts. Our head servant came weeping, "Madam," he said, "I have seen his wife, and his picture hangs in my house!" (Jackie shopped the bazaar on her visit.) M.A., PORTLAND, OR

9.

I Heard It on the Radio

DEAR ABBY: I was at a gas station filling my tank for my long drive home to Colorado when the attendant said, "Have you been listening to the radio? Have you heard? The president has been shot."

I didn't want to believe him. I had just left my fiance who was on a plane headed for Vietnam. I was numb. I couldn't help but wonder how this would affect our guys in Vietnam. I felt lost, alone, scared, and wondered how Thanksgiving could have much meaning that year.

That week in my life was probably one of the few weeks I'll remember in detail forever. I might add that the eleven-hundred-mile drive became a blur as the time flew while being glued to the radio.

L.M., PEPPERELL, MA

I heard the news on the car radio and initially thought it was a hoax (like "War of the Worlds"). The shock was so great that the significance didn't sink in for hours. B.Y.H., CHARLESTON, WV

Dear Abby . . .

I *was parked outside my son's school waiting to take him shopping. I turned on the radio just in time to hear the awful news.*

We went directly home that Friday. I never went to bed until Sunday night. I sat in front of our TV set. No meals were prepared. Fortunately, we had lunch meats and food of that sort.

On Sunday I saw Oswald murdered. I started laughing hysterically and called my neighbor. I said to her, "You'll never guess what just happened!" I realized that my state of mind was due to lack of sleep as well as the horror of it all. I'll **never** *forget that weekend!*

C.S.L., CHARLESTON HEIGHTS, SC

On November 22, 1963, I was at home just a few days after a radical mastectomy. I was lying down after lunch when the word came over the radio that Jack Kennedy had been shot. I was overwhelmed with apprehension and grief. I shall long remember.
J.S., COLUMBUS, OH

. . . I Heard It on the Radio

I was sitting in my car waiting for the traffic light to change. The news came on. The light turned green— no one budged. I sat up straight so I could look at the sky and ask, "Why God? Why?" Men of all ages, boys, girls—all walking with sobbing hearts. Men buried their heads on steering wheels, arms wrapped around the wheels. I could see shoulders racked with pain as we cried our eyes out for a president so well loved. No one moved for a good half hour. Sobs could be heard for blocks away. V.D., CLEVELAND, OH

When I heard that President Kennedy had been shot, I was standing at the sink washing dishes in Ottawa, Canada. I called my husband at the American Embassy, which was then in Ottawa, and told him what I'd heard on the radio. He said I must be mistaken because they had not heard it at the embassy. P.J., WACO, TX

I worked in a Cadillac car dealership in Chicago and was just about ready to close the deal with a prince of a customer. He took two $100 bills out of his wallet and plunked them down on my desk saying, "Take that to make the deal official." Just at that very second the radio in the back office announced, "A special report, a special report, the president has been shot in Dallas, Texas." With that my customer cried, "Oh my God, oh my God." He grabbed the $200 and his hat, and ran out. K.F., CORPUS CHRISTI, TX

T he radio was on. My ears heard, "The president has been shot. The motorcade is speeding toward Parkland Hospital."

There was utter chaos on the station and the country for the rest of the day. It was not my first presidential election I had voted in, BUT HE WAS MY FIRST PRESIDENT. J.O., HURON, SD

I *was diving in one hundred feet of water on the ocean bottom offshore in Santa Barbara, California. The news about the president came over the diver's radio to me on the bottom of the ocean.*

G.C., ANCHORAGE, AL

O ur family was gathered in the living room of my home awaiting the funeral cars to escort us to the burial service for my mother. The radio and TV were silent in respect of the occasion. But my ten-year-old daughter slipped upstairs to her room and quietly listened to her radio. A few minutes later she burst into the room saying, "President Kennedy's been shot!" We heard the news confirmed just as the funeral vehicles arrived. We left my home with increased sadness. An ironic aftermath occurred when just six months later this same little girl was dead of a heart ailment. D.M.B., INDEPENDENCE, MO

I was in the waiting room of my psychiatrist's office slightly early for my appointment. I had a transistor radio with a silent attachment plugged into my ear. When I heard the shocking news, I ran to the desk girl and shouted, "The president has been shot!" She came out, calmly took my arm, led me into the doctor's office and asked the doctor to see me at once!

ST. LOUIS, MO

I was in a local laundromat when the news bulletin came over the radio. Everyone was stunned. As soon as I could leave, I went home, and until his funeral was over, I was almost glued to the television. E.H., DANVERS, MA

I was on my stepladder with my little radio on, painting the wood trim on our front porch when the news came on. I jumped off the ladder, ran in,

turned on the TV only to see Mrs. Kennedy crawling toward the trunk of the car with the president slumped over. I ran to my neighbors and told them to turn on their TV to any station. Then I ran back home and watched in horror as history unfolded.
R.M., DE LAND, FL

I was returning from the unemployment office and had stopped for a red light. I did not have my radio on, but coming from a gas station I heard, "The president's been shot." I wondered what president they were talking about, never thinking it was *our* president. L.M.G., SANTA MONICA, CA

After President Kennedy was killed, I remember the radio only played religious music all day long for every hour of the day. E.L., SEATTLE, WA

My daughter and I were in a jewelry store when the news on the radio told us of President Kennedy being shot. We took our purchase and found a church that was open. Although it wasn't ours, we went in to pray for him. Soon we noticed many more people coming in, I'm sure for that same purpose.
F.T.A., LOS ANGELES, CA

. . . I Heard It on the Radio

On that terrible morning, I was sitting in the dental chair in Revere, Massachusetts, when the radio interrupted the soothing music to announce that President Kennedy had been assassinated. I recently mentioned this to a young dental hygienist who apparently doubted my memory after all these years because later she said, "You were right. I looked in your records and this is where you were." I will *never* forget. M.S., MIDDLETON, MA

I was on my way to sign papers on the first home I bought when I heard on the radio that President Kennedy had been assassinated. When we arrived at the building in Lowell, Massachusetts, the lawyer was looking out the window and was very visibly shaken. He told me he had been Jack Kennedy's roommate in college, and he showed me a letter he had recently received from the president.

N.B., ATKINSON, NH

On November 22, 1963, I was in the Lincoln Tunnel, driving to New Jersey from New York City when I heard the news. I bumped into a big truck ahead of me and bashed in my car's front end. The repairman was sympathetic, saying he had repaired many car accidents caused by that news. He did not reduce the charges however. D.R.F., PROVO, UT

I was washing my first car, a 1951 Chevy. The radio was on the step ladder. The milkman was in the driveway next door. I was eighteen years old living in my hometown of Portsmouth, Ohio. E.B., ALLIANCE, NE

I had just returned from lunch with a colleague from Switzerland. A worker in an adjoining office had a radio on and he rushed in to tell us the news. We listened to the radio with shock and horror. My Swiss colleague exclaimed, "How could such a terrible thing happen in such a wonderful country?" R.D., WAYNE, NJ

I was in a store shopping for a radio for my husband for Christmas. The salesperson took a small radio from the shelf and turned it on. That first flash of the president's shooting came on. It's a moment I'll never forget. The sales person replaced the radio saying nothing, and I just walked out of the store in shock. R.B., CAMBRIDGE, OH

The day that President Kennedy was assassinated we were taking a test drive in a new car. When the announcement aired, my husband stopped pulling away from the curb, and we sat stunned for some time. E.A.T., LAKEWOOD, CO

At a restaurant in Pacific, Missouri, a waitress came running out of the kitchen agitatedly stammering that Walter Cronkite was crying on TV and telling the country that President Kennedy had been shot. The rest of our three-hundred-mile trip we listened with unbelief to radio updates and finally it sank in that he *really was gone.* Unforgettable! J.G., ST. ANN, MO

All hammering and sawing stopped and in disbelief we said, "What did he say?" The radio news was on and the five of us, my husband, three children, and myself were working on a room addition to our home. Work ceased for a few days as we mourned the untimely, tragic death of our president. J.P., ST. LOUIS, MO

I was out elk hunting that day south of Flagstaff, Arizona. When I got back to my car late that evening, I heard the news over the radio. That was really sad. I didn't even go out hunting any more. T.J., PHOENIX, AZ

On November 22, 1963, I was sitting in a car in Miami, Florida, being told by my husband that he had a girlfriend in Alaska. At that moment the news came over his car radio. I remember thinking, how ironic, we had both just lost our husband and I felt so sad for Jackie, but also for myself. C.D., PHILADELPHIA, PA

In October I received my "Greetings" from the president. I was ordered to report to the Army Induction Center in Ashland, Kentucky. I was standing in line with a group of other inductees. A sergeant had his radio playing when the report came through that President Kennedy had been killed.

J.E.B., MADISON HEIGHTS, VA

The news came over the car radio. I pulled over and cried. A police cruiser came up behind me and asked if I was okay. I told him President Kennedy was just shot and it looked bad. We listened for a while and the officer cried with me.

D.E.C., WALTHAM, MA

It was late morning. I was on the Providence to Barrington, Rhode Island, road after a class at Brown University. Suddenly the radio announced the president had been shot. After that the D.J. started playing "Nearer My God to Thee." U.C., LIVINGSTON, MT

I was in New York City walking up Fifth Avenue. Traffic was a mess and noisy. Then, like in a dream, everything got real quiet. Taxis, cars, buses, trucks—everything froze in place. You could hear on the radios, "The president has been shot." Then he was dead. Everyone stopped. We cried together, strangers on the street, crying for one of our family.

G.C.W., OAKLAND, CA

10.

It Was My Birthday

DEAR ABBY: *November 22, 1963, was my thirteenth birthday. I was sitting in my Social Studies class daydreaming—after all I was now a* teen*!*

The announcement came over the loudspeaker that President Kennedy had been shot. I'll never forget the silent moments that followed or the cries and panic that took place in the hallways shortly thereafter.

Others may have forgotten the day they became a teenager—I never will. It was a day of passage from childhood to the adult world—a very visual one.

S.M., CHITTENANGO, NY

I was a five-year-old little girl from Scotch Plains, New Jersey, who asked her mother why everyone was coming to my birthday party crying! C.F.A., DUBLIN, OH

My son was born that day. The nurse told me later that there were eighteen boys born that day, and at least half were named after the deceased president.*

J.L.L., ST. LOUIS, MO

I t was my day off from work (at a drug store) and also my fifty-third birthday. My husband came in and said, "Kennedy was shot." I said, "Which one, Angus or Hugh?" (They were brothers and our friends; it was also hunting season.) I was told it was our President Kennedy. Every birthday I think of the assassination. N.T., GRANGEVILLE, ID

M y birthday is November 21, my daughter's is November 23. We did not hold our usual birthday celebration that year. We mourned our great loss. R.N., DELMAR, NY

I was not here when President Kennedy was shot. I was born after President Kennedy was shot and before President Johnson was sworn in. There was no President of the United States when I came into the world! T.P., MAPLE LAKE, MN

I was in Las Vegas celebrating my fifty-eighth birth-day when my wife told me that Kennedy had been shot. As word was passed around, the city went into mourning. P.O., TEMPLE CITY, CA

O n November 22, 1963, my husband and I were eat-ing dinner at Oscar's in Jefferson City, Missouri. It

was my twenty-first birthday, and I just found out
that I was pregnant with our first child. What a day!
B.E., ST. LOUIS, MO

It was my nineteenth birthday and I was studying
in the women's lounge at the University of Dayton,
Ohio, when someone came in and said, "The president
has been shot." While we all sat there in shock, the
church bells began to ring in the slow mournful
sound and we knew he had died. All classes were
canceled. It was the worst birthday ever.
M.A.S., BEAVERCREEK, OH

November 22 was my wife's birthday. Our two
children, then ages five and three, could not
understand why Mommy and Daddy were eating
birthday cake and crying. HILTON HEAD, NC

I had just successfully passed through my mother's
birth canal. What a day! K.A., MT. PLEASANT, SC

I was frosting a cake for my oldest son's eighth
birthday. When my children came home and told me
they heard the news in school, my oldest daughter
asked, "Why did he have to be killed on Ronald's
birthday?" BATAVIA, NY

Dear Abby . . .

I *was in the delivery room when I heard that JFK had been shot. He died before my son was born. It was a sad time in the hospital, but still a happy one for me. My son is now an engineer and works at Kennedy Space Center.*

B.M., PATERSON, NJ

I was not alive on November 22, 1963. I was born on November 22, 1969, and for the last twenty-four years I have felt as if I were born in the shadow of JFK's assassination. Every year on my birthday the lead news story begins, "X years ago JFK was killed and America mourned." Are we still in mourning? It was a terrible day in our history, one which many people will never forget. But must we continue to make such a production of grieving? It won't bring him back. GLEN ELLYN, IL

On November 22, 1963, I turned "Sweet 16." The chilling announcement that President Kennedy had been assassinated came over the intercom. Suddenly my sixteenth birthday seemed insignificant. Prayer in schools was allowed then so we prayed for Mrs. Kennedy and the family.

School dismissed early and most businesses closed, including the driver's license bureau. I had to wait a week to get my license. D.K.B., KENOSHA, WI

The day President Kennedy was shot was my thirty-third birthday. I was baking a cake for my husband and six children. After hearing the news on the radio, I didn't feel much like frosting the cake or celebrating. E.F., WEST CALDWELL, NJ

It was my fifteenth birthday. Being a typical selfish teenager, my first thought was, "Oh no, my mom's going to make me cancel my party." Of course she did and I've always felt a little guilty for thinking of myself first. I always remember the date.
C.J., NORTHBROOK, IL

I was in third grade. My mother had planned a birthday party for me. I was too young to realize the importance of what had happened in Dallas. I was just a little girl in Amarillo that didn't get to celebrate. AMARILLO, TX

Giving birth is a very traumatic time for a woman, but on that day I was almost ashamed to be in labor. I was

watching "As the World Turns" when the announcer cut in with the tragic news from Dallas. We heard the words, "One is dead, and one is wounded!" I didn't have time to stay tuned.

On the way to the hospital I saw the flags in downtown Minneapolis were at half-staff. We then knew that John Kennedy was dead.

As we arrived at the hospital, I saw a group of people around the TV in the lobby. I watched there for a little while until the nurse came to get me. She thought because I was crying that I was in very intense labor and yelled for everyone to get out of the way. Actually, in all the trauma, my labor had stopped. I was the only person in the labor room. They let me have my radio, unheard of in those days. All the personnel came in to listen. After my son was born I noticed a lot of the babies in the nursery were named John or Kennedy. I still find it hard to write about that day.

B.S., BROOKLYN PARK, MN

. . . It Was My Birthday

I had just returned from signing up at my local draft board when I heard the president had been shot. It was my eighteenth birthday! B.S., SAN ANTONIO, TX

When I got to work on the morning of November 22, 1963, I was surprised by my coworkers with a birthday cake and gifts. It turned out to be my worst birthday ever. I will never forget what happened on that day thirty years ago. C.K., SAFETY HARBOR, FL

On November 22, 1963, I celebrated my sweet sixteenth birthday. I remember that day like it was yesterday. Back then a girl wore a big corsage with sugar cubes on it.

It was Friday, about 2:00 p.m. While I was in typing class the message that President Kennedy was shot was made over the loudspeaker. Everyone in class just sat quietly until they realized what happened.

After school I went home and my party turned into a memorial for President Kennedy. Everyone cried. Each year I know exactly how many years President Kennedy has been dead. It's not hard to figure out. D.S., STATEN ISLAND, NY

It was my twelfth birthday and I had a slumber party that night. All of my girlfriends and I sat around the TV set and cried. M.A.N., HUNTINGTON, WV

My son David was born eight minutes before the terrible shooting. My husband heard the news on the waiting room TV. I was barely aware of what was happening and the nurses *never* talked about it to the new mothers. Obviously, my son will be thirty on November 22! A.R., PLAINFIELD, IN

That day happened to be my twenty-seventh birthday, and I remember having no appetite for the cake and ice cream my husband brought home that night. Each year the memory is just as vivid. BLOOMINGTON, IL

I walked into the kitchen to find my mother taking down the "Happy Birthday" sign. She had been crying and she said that no one would be coming to my party because the president had been shot and everyone was sad. I was amazed that so many people knew the president well enough to be upset. I thought he must be pretty special. I felt sad, too. J.L., HOLBROOK, LONG ISLAND

I count my years by each anniversary of the Kennedy assassination. Can it really have been thirty years? E.J., EL SEGUNDO, CA

11.

I Was at Work

DEAR ABBY: I was at my desk in the Rayburn House Office Building, Washington, D.C., where I could see the flag being lowered to half-mast and wondering who it was for. When the news came in, I experienced the most traumatic reaction I can remember in my lifetime. H.G., PALM CITY, FL

When our President Kennedy was shot I was operating a Linotype in Hillsdale, Michigan. With tears blurring my eyes, I continued typing news bulletins until nightfall. J.B., LARGO, FL

I *was working in a nursing home. A sweet lady of ninety-two was about to faint. I held her and she said, "Why wasn't it me? I'm of no more use. He was so great, so young, and could do so much good."*

FAYETTEVILLE, AR

I *worked in New York City, but as a native Texan, my car had a Texas license plate. That night my car windows were smashed!*

M.G., HOLMDEL, NJ

. . . I Was at Work

A s a patrol officer with the Los Angeles Police Department, I was writing a motorist a traffic violation at a busy intersection when a large truck suddenly stopped next to me and shouted, "They shot Kennedy in Dallas!" During the remainder of that day, I saw hundreds of citizens walking and driving in an obvious state of shock, violating virtually every section of the vehicle code. Needless to say, my citation book remained in my pocket until my shift ended.
L.S., BONSALL, CA

I am a Hungarian-German who came to the U.S. with my parents after World War II. I campaigned for my beloved president and have a signed picture. When he was shot I was at work at Challenge Tool Co. in Indianapolis. They announced his death on the loudspeaker. We were in shock. F.H., KNIGHTSTOWN, IN

I was in my law office, a tough former judge and prosecutor, strong but fair. I cried like a baby.

J.T., UNION CITY, NJ

I was working as a drill press operator. One of my coworkers yelled that the president had been assassinated. I reacted by squeezing the air hose caus-

129

ing the metal chips to fly every which way, even putting one in my eye. The day of the funeral I watched TV with a patch on my eye, but that didn't keep the tears from rolling down my face. B.H., WARMINSTER, PA

I heard the report of the assassination while in President Kennedy's helicopter, sitting in *his* seat, and listening on *his* phone. I was a foreman at Sikorsky Aircraft and one of his helicopters was going through its annual overhaul. I can never forget. J.D., VENTURA, CA

I had just completed reading Walt Whitman's "O Captain, My Captain," written in memory of President Lincoln's assassination, to my sixth grade class. The memory of this strange coincidence still raises many feelings. T.W., ALFORD, MA

Two weeks before, I had taken ill during the school day and the principal, Bob Johnson, was pressed into finishing the day in my first grade classroom. In searching for a way to explain the assassination and let the children know their world would continue pretty much as usual I was able to say, "Do you remember when Mrs. Kennedy got sick and had to leave and Mr. Johnson came in and finished teaching the lessons? Well, John Kennedy won't be able to be our president anymore and a different Mr. Johnson will take over for him." I.L.K., HACIENDA HEIGHTS, CA

I was a long-distance operator for Mountain Bell Telephone. Our switchboards were overloaded the first hour, then absolutely dead for the next four. People were watching their televisions, too shocked to phone. B.B., SANDY, UT

When President Kennedy was shot, I was carrying mail in Graham, North Carolina. I was at the corner of Holt Avenue and Green Street. Someone came out onto their porch and told me. It seemed as if everything was so quiet and still. No birds singing and no noise of any kind. R.M., HAW RIVER, NC

The day President Kennedy was assassinated, I was driving a truck hauling soybeans from Texhoma, Oklahoma, to Plainview, Texas. When I drove on the scales to weigh the soybeans a fellow ran out and told me. It was very devastating indeed. I liked him and he was an intelligent president. I'm eighty years old but it still is a vivid scene yet. G.G.F., TEXHOMA, OK

I was an eighteen-year-old dental assistant in a rural Los Angeles suburb. When news came that JFK had

131

been shot, the patient in the chair (an astrology buff) said she wasn't surprised, "It was in his chart."
LOS ANGELES, CA

I was on an assembly line at Zenith Radio in Sioux City, Iowa. The news came over a test radio and spread like wildfire. Everyone was just heartsick and wanted the assembly line to shut down so we could absorb the shock, but they wouldn't do it.
D.W., SAINT CLOUD, MN

> *It was very personal to me. I frequently saw the president returning to the White House after his weekly press conference. He always returned my wave. I'll never forget.*
>
> B.L., NORTH BEACH, MD

I was working at 120 Broadway in New York. Outside on Nassau Street, a large Rolls-Royce was parked with the radio on full blast, as crowds gathered to listen to the news. Everyone seemed to know instantly—like it was not possible to tell someone—the news spread so fast. Then, when the news came that JFK was dead, the bells in Trinity Church started to toll.

Later, I fished out of the wastebasket the Dow-Jones newstape of the day—thrown out angrily by

someone sick of the day's news. I still have it, probably a very rare memento—the whole story from start
to finish on paper as it was broadcast by Dow-Jones to
news tickers across the U.S.A. R.W.Z., NEW YORK, NY

I was showing a baby for adoption in a children's
home. The new parents and I stood in shock. What
should have been a joyful occasion had that sadness
attached to it. I'm sure, after all these years, their
memory of that day is as vivid as mine. A.S., HOMEWOOD, IL

My husband and I looked forward to November 22,
1963, because it meant after years of scrimping
and saving we were opening our own retail business.
Our grand opening lasted about two hours because we
closed our doors in respect and sorrow at the passing
of a great man.

We kept our business twenty-five years and always
remembered our first day. R.K., NAPLES, FL

I was teaching ninth graders science that day. We
were encouraged to continue our lessons as a trib-
ute to President Kennedy. There was shock but *no*
hysteria. My tears came later. S.T., DENVER, CO

On November 22, 1963, as a costumer
on the "Danny Kaye Show" at CBS,

Dear Abby . . .

*I was preparing for rehearsal. Mahalia
Jackson, guest star on the show, came
in crying and said, "They shot my
president!" We sat together holding and
consoling each other for a long, long
time. The rehearsal was canceled. I don't
remember what she sang on the show.
The world was changed—the show and
life went on.*

A.W.E., VENICE, CA

I was sitting at my desk typing a letter at Kelly Air
Force Base. What makes it so bad is President Kennedy had just arrived at Kelly earlier, and I chose not
to go out and greet him. Since I am in a wheelchair,
I thought I would be in the way. I will never forgive
myself. F.E., SAN ANTONIO, TX

I was teaching kindergarten in Orrville, Ohio. Imme-
diately after a moment of silence, I said, "Amen."
One little sharp fellow said, "Well, it wasn't John
Wilkes Booth that did it." H.L., DOVER, OH

U pon leaving work that day, the normally active
downtown was like a funeral procession. Everyone

on the buses simply stared out the windows on their way home from work. S.B., KNOXVILLE, TN

I was working in a cafeteria. In March that year I had lost my only son, nineteen years old, in a car accident. As I heard the terrible news, all I could do all that day was to say over and over, that poor mother. I was so sorry for her. It's so terrible to lose a child. D.N., PHOENIX, AZ

As a freelance writer for the movie magazines, I was driving down Sunset Boulevard. I had an appointment to interview Jayne Mansfield. My car was an open convertible with a broken radio. I noticed cars all around were pulling over to the sides of the streets. I stopped along side of one and was told the devastating news! This was thirty years ago, but it seems like yesterday. E.N., DELRAY BEACH, FL

I was working in Washington, D.C., in the Main Treasury Building—directly across the street from the White House. From my office window, I could see Caroline and John John Kennedy playing on the lawn; I could see Macaroni the pony, and watched the presidential

helicopter land and take off every Friday.
On November 22, on a long-distance call,
all lines went dead. We got the message
that the president had been shot. I stood
at my office window and watched the flag
on top of the White House. Before
anyone knew that the president was dead,
I saw the White House flag lowered. I
knew that he had died. Now, thirty years
later, I work for the Peace Corps.

E.L.R., OVERLAND PARK, KS

I was an Alabama State Trooper at the time we were alerted to President Kennedy's assassination. There was a belief that the assassinations could be nationwide on all our leaders so there was a mad scramble to locate then Governor George Wallace who was in Tuscaloosa shopping with his family. S.M., CHILDERSBURG, AL

A s an elementary school teacher in Rock Island, Illinois, we briefly discussed the government's provision for the transfer of power to the vice-president, and then I suggested we pray for the Kennedy family and our country's future. The unity and calmness it created in my classroom is a feeling I'll never forget. B.S., ROCK ISLAND, IL

I was employed by Illinois Bell Telephone as a long-distance operator. When the news broke our boards lit up like a Christmas tree. M.L., ARKANSAS

I was a classmate of John Kennedy,
Harvard 1940, and was shocked when
I heard in my office in Miami, Florida,
that he had been shot. I rushed home to
confirm the sad news on TV. It was a
big turning point in the American
political scene.

R.R., MANILA, PHILIPPINES

I was a receptionist in a doctor's office
when the news came on the TV. Later
that day, a lonely stray kitten came into
the doctor's office. It was a pretty tiger
kitty. I took him home with me and
called him "Fitzgerald."

D.S., SEDAN, KS

On that fateful day in November, I was with my usual lunch bunch in the Department of State's cafeteria. All of a sudden it was a different day. We noticed people running into the cafeteria, and more people than usual hurriedly leaving. It was all done very quietly—no public address announcement. We did notice it seemed to be people from the top echelon of the department. When I returned to my office my wife called to say President Kennedy had been shot. At 1:30 a.m. I was awakened by the phone. Report to the office immediately to look for correspondence from Oswald. H.L.S., MCLEAN, VA

I was assisting in a major surgery when a nurse came into the O.R. to report the president was dead. The head surgeon said, "I never agreed with his politics, but in America we don't do things this way." T.D., SEATTLE, WA

Early November 22, 1963, I was very sad because I was being laid off my job. Imagine how I felt upon learning later in the afternoon about the president's assassination. I remember saying, "I lost my job and the country lost its president." A.K., CHICAGO, IL

Fresh out of high school, I was hauling parts up and down the main assembly line at Farmall Tractor Plant, joking and laughing with the assembler. When I heard the news, the laughter fell right off my face, tears filled my eyes, and those parts suddenly became the heaviest things I'd ever handled in my life. J.C.A., SILVIS, IL

12.

I'll Always Remember

DEAR ABBY: Thank you for remembering. We all do. Like the end of World War II, lots of tears and heartaches. G.T., HELENA, MT

I was thirteen, in the eighth grade in Astoria, Oregon. John Kennedy had been to our small town only a short time before to dedicate the Tongue Point Job Corps Center, the first of its kind. I had the privilege of shaking his hand as he swept past hundreds of us that day.

As only a sentimental, adolescent girl would, I saved his special "germs" in a jar. On the afternoon of November 22, I put them in a flag-draped shoebox and buried them on a quiet hillside in Astoria. Then I sat down and cried.

G.C.H., PORTLAND, OR

We were learning part of a poem for our "Words of Wisdom" for the day. I will always remember the poem in reference to John Kennedy, and all his good qualities.

Not gold, but only man
Can make a nation great and strong . . .
Stand fast and suffer long. J.L.L., LONG BEACH, CA

. . . I'll Always Remember

I was standing beside the hospital bed of my grandmother holding her hand as she died. I cried because I was left without her and I cried for a country left without a leader. B.P., HARDEEVILLE, SC

It seems impossible that thirty years have passed since that horrifying day. The world was in shock and saddened, a lovely lady was widowed, two little children lost their father, and a nation lost our president.

But through Civil Rights, the Space Program, Medicare, and the Peace Corps, we will always remember and miss him. S.M., INDIANAPOLIS, IN

As you know, Kennedy's body lay in state in the rotunda of the Capitol Building. My husband and I lived six blocks from there. People were lined for blocks all day long and into the night to view his body. About 3:00 a.m. the next morning, I awoke to an odd sound outside the front of our house. A line of people walking two and three abreast, stretched from the Capitol Building as far as we could see. There wasn't a sound except for the shuffling feet. It's

*something I can never forget. Deaths in
the family have been very painful to
experience, but the shuffling feet of
thousands in the middle of the night is
the most solemn memory.*

L.O., LIVERMORE, CA

On Monday I called my boss and told him I
wouldn't be in, as I was too upset, and not to
expect me in until after the funeral. My wife was
very understanding, and I don't know if our two
small children knew why their dad was crying. My
job was waiting for me and my boss paid me for all
lost time. M.G., QUINCY, IL

I don't think this country has ever been the same.
H.C., ORMOND BEACH, FL

I am eighty-six years old and I shall never forget.
President Kennedy's death hit me especially hard
because I had had the privilege of knowing him
personally. Arkansas Congressman Wilbur Mills had
introduced me to the president and recommended me
as a member of a special health committee that was
being formed at that time. President Kennedy was a
very special *gentle man.* R.R., NEW ORLEANS, LA

I was in eighth grade English, diagramming sentences. I sat by the window, third row from the front. I remember *no* other classrooms from junior high school, but *that* one is imprinted in my memory.
S.B., EUGENE, OR

It was hard to believe we were witnessing something as historic as the assassination of President Lincoln. I hope we learn the whole truth (in my lifetime) about what really happened that tragic day.
D.P., AUSTIN, TX

I was eating my lunch and watching "Lunch with Casey." Years later when removing old wallpaper from the room I was in, we discovered my older brother had written that date on the wall behind the mirror. P.S., ST. PAUL, MN

I was in ninth grade at Van Nuys High school. I'll never forget what I was wearing that day: peacock blue sweater and matching skirt—"Bobbie Brooks," and brand-new patent-leather black-and-white saddle shoes—all the rage at that moment. I never wore those shoes again. Imagine recalling this some thirty years later. What a terrible time that was. J.T., ENCINO, CA

143

Dear Abby . . .

When I reached my grandmother's house, all my relatives were there, pacing, crying, worrying, and watching the TV. Dabbing her eyes, I remember Aunt Mamie saying, "Things will never be the same for us" (meaning Blacks). BAD KREUZNACH, GERMANY

My recollections are not unique. Every American rabbi experienced the same hours of numbed scrambling upon hearing the terrible word, and observed the same outpouring of feeling that overflowed synagogues that Friday evening, that feeling which also overflowed churches that Sunday.

One suspects that only those of us then alive and aware truly know how it felt to be American citizens on November 22, 1963. D.H.R., KINSTON, NC

When our youngest son was born in 1962, we bought a "Kennedy" rocking chair.

And then those awful words, "President Kennedy is dead." I remember it as yesterday. I rocked and cried, gently stroking the maple wood arms of the chair, as if for comfort and consolation.

It doesn't go with anything else in our home now, but I just cannot seem to part with my "Kennedy" rocker. M.M., ARLINGTON, TX

I think this was the most profoundly traumatic event of our generation. I

144

*was in my late twenties and everyone
I knew has said the same thing. Re-
gardless of the scandals that surfaced
later, he was the last president who
made us feel that we could change
things in the world. Many people I
knew, young and old, signed up for the
Peace Corps and did other things that
were inspired by John Kennedy.*

S.J.L., WILMINGTON, CA

I was only ten months old. I only know what people have told me. I was told that he was a very good president and a good person, and that he was liked by everyone. So, can someone tell me why he was assassinated? Who wanted this powerful, well-loved man dead? They don't teach us enough about him in school. I find his life to be fascinating and yet so sad. He had everything, and it all ended so fast. It seems so unfair. Only the good die young. BAGLEY, MN

I still feel the loss as if a member of my family had been killed. I was twenty years old that year and just about idolized John Kennedy. I don't think I will ever forget. M.B., GADSDEN, AL

I had gone to the Middlebury College library to escape the distraction of the dormitory. I don't remember the rest of that dark afternoon. I guess we all went to our rooms; I guess we all ate dinner. A lot of us went to church. But that evening, all of us, far from our families, had the same thought: Call home.

We lined up in the hall to use the dorm phones, standing, sitting on the floor, as diverse a group of young women as there could be. We were poor kids on scholarships, millionaires' daughters, from farms and penthouses, nearby towns and faraway continents. But we all had something in common.

In every town and city we called, the church bells were slowly tolling. And on a day when we all felt very much alone, we really were very much together.

H.B.H., RUTLAND, VT